STRASBOURG

the European

STRAS

BOURG
the European

Marie-Christine Périllon

Translated from the French
by Ken Kincaid

hoëbeke

© 2003, Éditions Hoëbeke, Paris
Published August 2003
ISBN : 2-84230-182-X

Design and artwork by Massin
Visual research by Bénédicte Mathey
Production by Thierry Renard
Proof-read by LTA-Tradweb

Printed in France by **Partenaires-Livres**® (JL)

1

Impressionist Portrait

"This pink is a delicate, muted pink whose patina is more like that of wood than of stone; the trunk of the eucalyptus tree is sometimes that colour."
Mario Praz

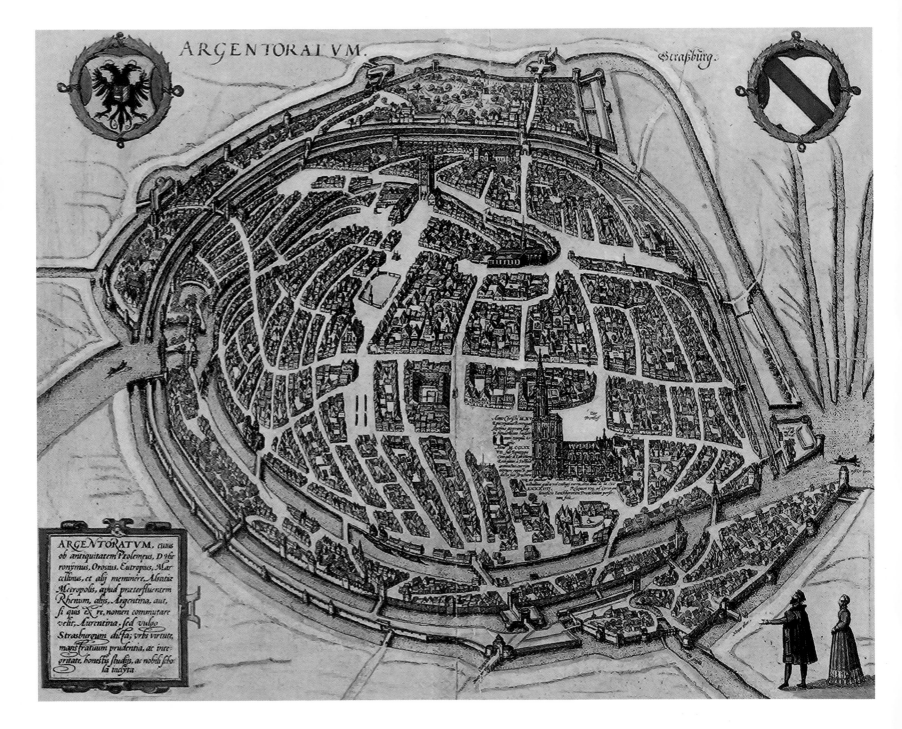

ARGENTORATVM.   Straßburg.

ARGENTORATVM, cuius
ob antiquitatem Ptolemeus, D Hie
ronymus, Orosius, Eutropius, Mar
cellinus, et alij meminere, Alsatiæ
Metropolis, apud præterfluentem
Rhenum, alijs, Argentina, aut,
si quis & re, nomen commutare
velit, Aurentina, sed vulgo
Strasburgum dicta; urbis virtute,
magistratuum prudentia, ac inte
gritate, honestis studijs, ac nobili scho
la inclyta

Strasbourg is a fine example of a city that was laid out to
the original Roman plan and organised around a waterway,
as this 1572 map shows.

8

In his novel, "Aurelien", the great French poet and novelist, Louis Aragon, wrote lyrically of the infinite greys of Paris. Strasbourg boasts infinite hues of pink – from the pink patina of the cathedral to the unruly rose-pink of its half-timbered houses festooned with geraniums. And when light plays on the pinks, the light so characteristic of the cities of Mitteleuropa, at times dazzling and radiant, at others subdued and mysterious, the effect is truly magical. To appreciate it, stroll across the square outside the purple-pink cathedral on a sunny day, or sit of a summer's evening under the glass canopy and glinting marble of the Palais Universitaire's *Aula*, or lecture hall. Or cross the bridge of Saint-Nicolas when the medieval gables of the Ancienne Douane (Old Customs House) merge into the lowering sky on an early winter morning. In Strasbourg water acts like a doppelganger. It mirrors the astounding variety of architectural styles, like a graceful compendium of centuries past. Some buildings, like the Ancienne Grande Boucherie (Old Slaughterhouse) or the Palais Rohan, stand back from the river, as if putting the distance of a courtyard or terrace between them and it. The small half-timbered houses of the Petite France neighbourhood are anything but stand-offish. They stand on the very edge of the river which churns past out of the sluice gates. Their pastel shades of pink, blue, yellow and green tremor in the water like some shimmering rainbow.

Water, water, everywhere…

It is impossible to lose one's way in central Strasbourg. Should you happen to wander off the beaten track, the waters of the River Ill will bring you up short like a taut wire marking a border. When you come to the end of a street, a bridge will always hove into view as if to say, "here you leave the old city crowded with half-timbered houses, churches and palaces". Strasbourg is an island clasped in the arms of the River Ill. The Ill rises in the southern Alsatian region of Sundgau, flows in a long straight line, then describes a loop that girdles the city – the last fling of a tame little river before it reaches its journey's end and runs into the Rhine well outside Strasbourg at the town of La Wantzenau.

The city's central island stands on peat marshland where, in 12 BC, the Romans established a military camp, one of a long string of *castella* which Drusus, one of Emperor Augustus's stepsons built on the banks of the Rhine. The Romans drained, filled and dried the marsh to build Argentoratum, or the "Silver Fortress". The camp had a turbulent history before it was finally destroyed by the Huns in the 5th century and was reborn under the name of Strateburgum, "the city of roads". The city centre, where the cathedral now stands, once resounded to the martial steps of soldiers from the 8th Roman Legion on their way to the temple, the bathhouse or the blade factory, all within the camp's walls. To do their shopping, they would head out of the military precinct for the "high street" where a motley mixture of craftsmen and merchants, generally from Greece and the Middle East, had their *cannabae*, or little shops. The Roman camp and its two thoroughfares, the traders' high street and praetorian way (now respectively the Rue du Dôme and Rue des Hallebardes), make up the backbone of the city's topography. Strasbourg was to grow in five successive bursts, all related to its riverside location. The river had always afforded the city natural fortification. This was further strengthened during the second period of growth, between 1202 and 1220, when a fortified mound with battlements was erected in a channel of the Ill. Today, all that remains is its name, the Canal du Faux Rempart (Channel of the False Rampart).

The name has an intriguing ring for the visitor strolling along the banks of the river, as does the name of the Opéra aux Ponts Couverts (Opera of the Covered Bridges), where the bridges have no roofs to be seen. It was during the city's third period of expansion, between 1228 and 1334 that the covered bridges were built. But just as battlements no longer

etching by Wenceslas Hollar entitled "Summer" depicts the bridges with their wooden roofs overhanging Woerthel Canal, in which swimmers splash happily. Another view is that of the Romantic painter, George Jones, who in 1850 showed the medieval towers in the foreground reflected in the peaceful mirror of the Ill where anglers fished contentedly. A postcard from 1900 reconstitutes the covered bridges and footbridge passing under Vauban's lock-dam to the Matthis bathhouse, much prized by the people of Strasbourg.

The waterfront vista has also inspired such contemporary writers as the Italian philosopher and art critic Mario Praz. In his book "This World As I Have Seen It", he writes : "One looks out from the Opera aux Ponts Couverts at an angle that could belong to the world which Vermeer immortalised in a celebrated view of Delft. If one turns one's back to the three sturdy turrets of the old ramparts which straddle the river at this point, one gazes at an enchanting little panorama of canals between spits of land whose ends abutt the covered bridges. The houses with their tall roofs, of a red deepening to brown, with numerous skylights, are plashed by tranquil, greenish waters of the first canal and their balconies are garnished with pink geraniums."

Praz's view has not changed, but has been augmented by some very contemporary buildings. The panorama that unfolds from the terrace atop Vauban's lock takes in not only the gables of the old city, spires like those of the astonishing Saint-Pierre-le-Vieux with its Catholic and Protestant steeples, the clocktower of Commanderie Saint-Jean, but also the long black silhouette of the Hôtel du Département (local government hall), which the architect Vasconi designed as a great liner mooring on the banks of the Ill. On the opposite bank another modern building, Adrien Fainsilber's Museum of Modern and Contemporary Art, echoes the ship-like Hôtel du Département, whose figurehead is Mimmo Paladino's strange masked horse. The concourse fronting the museum slopes gently down to the river. It has become one of the most popular meeting points in a

rise from the river, so the bridges have lost their roofs. They were finally lopped off in the 18th century.

Before then, however, they must have been picturesque and had something of Florence's Ponte Vecchio. The bridges were also a crucial part of the city's defensive system, principally because of their three turrets, which still stand today. Louis XIV's military engineer, Seigneur de Vauban, grasped their importance. When Strasbourg surrendered to the king in 1681, Vauban added another line of defence by building a fortified lock-dam.

The Mirror Effect

Today the view from the dam is one of Strasbourg's finest. Lithographers, painters and photographers have featured it in their works over the centuries. A 1630

city whose development is more than ever inseparable from the Ill, the Rhine and its canals. Water has been integral to the projects that have been changing the face of the city in the first years of the 21st century.

Strasbourg Grande Ile

In 1988 UNESCO added the historical heart of the city of Strasbourg, Strasbourg Grande Ile, to its World Heritage List, on a par with Venice and Prague. The very name of the Grande Ile (Big Island) conjures up water. So, too, do even older quarters, like Elsau, Ganzau, Meinau, Robertsau and Krutenau. Their "-au" suffix means "flood plain". Krutenau in particular played a decisive role in the city's history. Through it once ran the Rheingiessen, an offshoot of the Rhine, which flowed into the Ill near the church of Saint-Guillaume. It was an excellent waterway for transporting goods and people. The Romans used it to carry stones to build their camp

even before it was used for trade. In 1576 the people of Zurich ferried a steaming cauldron of millet down the Rheingiessen to Strasbourg as part of a test run to see how fast they could come to the rescue of their Strasbourg friends. The Rheingiessen was finally covered over in 1872. Until that time it was a genuine water boulevard in a neighbourhood inhabited chiefly by fishermen and boatmen. It is difficult to imagine nowadays that the Place de Zurich was more like a lake than a square! Only the so called "Zurichois" fountain is there as a reminder of the past and the gesture of friendship of the people of Zurich.

In the traditional old quarter of Petite France water is truly omnipresent. The Alsatian bards, the Matthis brothers, sang a song in dialect about the old plane tree that grew like a palm tree from paradise by the Pont du Péage (Toll Bridge). Only pleasure boats and launches now ply the shipping canal for which toll was taken, but the plane tree is still there. When the weather is

fine it is just the place to sip a drink in the shade of its leaves. The waterways no longer drive any mills, but some of them are etched in memory like the Würtzmuhle, or spice mill, whose very name conjures up the scents of cardamom, cinnamon and cloves. The 19th century saw mills give way to factories. One is still remembered for its smell – the Schall chocolate factory, which now stands outside the city limits.

Until that time, however, Petite France was not exactly reputed for its fragrance. The pungent odours of the skin trade could be smelled from afar. Although the city owes to the tanners its pretty houses with wide-vented roofs that were used for drying hides, tanning was an evil smelling business. When the 19th century poet Gerard de Nerval said in 1838 that Strasbourg had an overstrong air of the Middle Ages, perhaps he meant it literally! Two years later the tanners' gutter, which carried most of the foul waste material out of Petite France and through the city centre, was covered over.

Enchanting houses

Petite France today boasts the densest concentration of half-timbered houses in Strasbourg. They once belonged to craftsmen – sparse and sober dwellings whose gables described geometric figures like squares and rectangles. The more affluent houses had Saint Andrew's crosses with jig-sawed ends. In a passage from "Burghers and Soldiers" the great German novelist, Alfred Döblin, describes the timeless appeal of the houses in these terms: "Strasbourg was as beautiful and charming as ever. Old, half-timbered houses gazed at their reflections in the water and found them as fetching as two hundred years before. 'We haven't aged a day,' they would say each day at dawn."

Their facades are no longer whitewashed with the same monochrome, uniform cob, but are repainted as they originally were – bright blues, gleaming pinks and flaming ochres. These vivid, merry facades gradually fade to pastel with time.

Most of the houses rest on medieval bases, while their half-timbered upper floors date back to the 16th and 17th centuries. The oldest have oriel windows, which overhang the street below. An inscription in German, "Das is das Mass des Ueberhanges", (this is the mesurement of the overhang) spells out the exact size of oriels. It can be deciphered on the southern flank of the cathedral in front of which stands a statue of one of the cathedral's architects, Erwin de Steinbach.

It is in the Impasse de Bière that Strasbourg's two oldest private houses are to be found. On the corner of this cul-de-sac there once lived a certain Arnold, the city's biggest brewer, mention of whose name can be

found as early as the 12th century. Not far away, on Cathedral Square stands the most lavishly decorated half-timbered house of all – Kammerzell House. Made of wood, its 75 windows are all carved with icons from the Bible, mythology and history. Little pipers playing the fife or triangle gambol on its ledges, while the signs of the Zodiac, the five senses and a whole host of Biblical characters make the house into a sort of giant outdoor book. Haughty, monumental personifications of Faith, Hope and Charity rise like figureheads from the house's corners, prompting Mario Praz to write: "Next to the cathedral there is a house, Kammerzell House, which even Victor Hugo at his most Gothic could not have described."

The entrance level of Kammerzell House was built in 1467 as the inscription on the main door's lintel testifies. It is peerless among the city's half-timbered houses, even though some others, like Pigeon House and Crow's Yard Hotel, are fine examples in their own right. Visitors should make a point of going to the charming Place Saint-Etienne and strolling up the main drag of Grand-Rue to view some remarkable half-timbered houses like the Maison à l'Arc en Ciel (Rainbow House) and the Chasseur Magique (Magic Hunter).

Smiling Faces

With the exception of the outside of Kammerzell House, few carved wooden figures have weathered the test of time. The 17th century sought to offset the vulnerability of wood by scattering town houses with hundreds of graceful, intriguing stone faces.

An emblem of Catholicism's new-found glory in a city long dominated by Lutheranism is the magnificent twin-fronted palace, the Palais Rohan, built between 1730 and 1742. On one side it faces the cathedral, on the other the River Ill. The side facing the cathedral is alive with such sacred sculptures as that of Faith triumphantly branding its cross over the palace's main

Page left: The sheer wealth of decorative carvings on Kammerzell house decoration rivals with the cathedral's religious imagery.
Above: The walls of the Palais Rohan teem with smiling mascarons (left) as do those of the so-called "Poêle du Miroir" concert hall (right).

entrance. The façade looking out over the River Ill is studded with delicious profane carvings that evoke the court of the Cardinals of Rohan, a dynasty of four who succeeded each other as heads of the episcopal see of Strasbourg.

The allegory of Air in a series depicting the four elements is truly exquisite: a faint smile plays on the lips of a ravishing face crowned with peacock feathers. As unsettling as Air is exquisite, a grave, beautiful face under the chapel's entrance has the brooding feel of night. Ethereal Air and the dark, heavy-lidded beauty are just two of the works that make it worth visitors'

while to spend time seeing the palace and the wonderful museums it houses.

Mascarons (grotesque masks usually over a door or fountain), like those that peer from the Palais Rohan can be seen throughout the city dotting the facades of the stately town mansions which flourished in emulation of the Palais Rohan. A walk down the Rue Brûlée recalls Paris's Boulevard St-Germain for the sheer number of *hôtels particuliers*. There is the Hôtel du Préfet (formally that of the Royal Intendant Klinglin), the Hôtel du Gouverneur Militaire (formally Hôtel des Deux Ponts), the Bishop's Palace (formally Hôtel du Prévôt du Grand Chapitre), Hôtel de l'Abbé de Marmoutier, and the Hôtel de Ville, i.e. city hall (formally Hôtel des Hanau-Lichtenberg).

City hall receives the most visitors – hardly surprising as wedding ceremonies are held here in the vast mansion, which Napoleon donated to the city in return for the Palais Rohan. On the facade that gives on to the Place Broglie, a statue of Bacchus sporting a moustache and surrounded by women with flowers in their hair greets wedding parties. Ceremonies take place in rooms that have retained all the original elegance of their 18th century wainscoting.

Other buildings feature mascarons similar to those of the great town mansions. On the facade of the Poêle du Miroir concert hall where Mozart once performed, there is the head of a man topped with an elephant's trunk. It stands for Africa and is part of a suite devoted to the four continents. In Rue de l'Ecurie, the smiling faces of pretty damsels represent spring, summer and autumn and a stern, turbaned man winter.

Mitteleuropa feel

In the 18th century the steep, tiled roofs of Alsace gave way to mansard roofs. Palaces and stately homes were built from either pink or yellow sandstone. In the latter half of the next century the Franco-Prussian War put a stop to architectural alternation. Strasbourg, now a German city, was predominantly rebuilt with yellow sandstone. Urban planning and architectural ventures were designed to lend prestige to what was now the capital of the Reichsland of Alsace-Lorraine. The city's surface area tripled. Beautiful pastiches of the architecture of centuries past were on a colossal scale, epitomised by the Place de la République, a vast example of the Wilhelmian style. Standing in a circle around a French garden that gleams with the whiteness of magnolia in the spring and the gold of gingko trees in autumn five buildings unfold their Germanic majesty. One is the Palace of the Rhine, described as "elephantine" by Wilhelm I, who commissioned it. Under its great copper rooflight, libertine 18th century statuary gave way to squat Atlases, rippling with muscle and might. Visitors crossing the threshold of the palace catch their breath at the sheer size of the monumental entrance, with its triple staircase, orange marble fountains and glittering mosaic frescoes. The building today belongs partly to the Regional Government's Culture Department, which owns its most impressive section – the courtroom below the dome, where long rows of carmine red marble lead to a loggia that offers a magnificent view of the square. Opposite are the National Theatre of Strasbourg, once the seat of the Parliament of Alsace-Lorraine, and University Library, where students still come to pore over tomes in the hushed atmosphere of the dome of Reading Room 7.

On the other side of the Avenue de la Liberté, which once bore the name of Emperor Wilhelm, rises the most consummate example of the architecture of the time – the Palais Universitaire (University Palace). The sun at its zenith plunges through the glass canopy to flood the amphitheatre lecture hall in opalescent light. Vividly coloured centaurs in the corner spandrels compensate for the ancient plaster casts and Pompeian red fabric that once covered the walls, but are now relegated to the basement. On the roof of the palace are statues of such great thinkers as Kant, Paracelsus and Copernicus. Like angels from Wim Wenders's "Wings of Desire" they seem to watch over the new city with its wide thoroughfares and spacious parks.

Rearing from the Ile Sainte-Hélène as high and haughtily as a cathedral, the pale pink neo-Gothic Saint-Paul's Church dominates a vista that stretches to University Bridge. Cheek-by-jowl with the medieval town, the yellow sandstone town assumes capital city airs. The philosopher, Philippe Lacoue-Labarthe, who teaches at the University of Strasbourg, is keenly aware of how Strasbourg can evoke other times and other places: "The Palais Universitaire on a winter's evening is Berlin in 1930; story-telling on Yom Kippur night is Warsaw. At other times one suddenly finds oneself on the outskirts of Vienna, on the waterfront in a Hanseatic city or in Saint Petersburg in 1905. There is something of Prague in Strasbourg when the fog fails to lift for days on end and something of the monotonous beginnings of Mitteleuropa in the plain on the banks of the Rhine."

Jugendstil Touches

German Strasbourg is dotted with peculiar houses, some neo-Palladian, some neo-Gothic or neo-Renaissance and some even neo-rustic. Amid all these historical styles, a number of Jugendstil houses built between 1898 and 1905 add a touch of fantasy. Jugendstil was to Germany what Art Nouveau was to France, the Secessionist Style to Austria, the Modern Style to Britain and the Liberty Style to Italy. The names varied but all denoted the same international yearning to rejuvenate the plastic and decorative arts by drawing on organic shapes and forms of plants and

flowers. The buildings of Strasbourg are variations on themes from France, Germany and Austria and, as has always been the case, the confluence of these diverse influences yielded a wholly original result.

The oriel window, which had been a tradition since the Middle Ages, emerged from the Jugendstil period covered in exuberant plant-like carvings. The French balcony, which first appeared in the 18th century, was enriched with admirably rendered, crazy motifs. Over some balconies jutted the kind of canopy that is so typical of the wrought-iron Paris Metro entrances. One example is 22 Rue du Général de Castelnau.

Such dwellings have to be sought out. Take 76 Allée de la Robertsau, with its great sheaves of sunflowers spring up from beneath the windows of a majestic house. Visitors should also go out of their way to see the veranda strewn with irises at 22 Rue Sleidan, the beetle-shaped ironwork of the Egyptian villa at 10 Rue du Général Rapp, and the flower-bedecked oriel window of 22 Allée de la Robertsau. The School of Decorative Arts was founded in 1889. Its director, Anton Seder from Munich, vigorously encouraged the Jugendstil movement. Visitors should head for the Krutenau neighbourhood and take a stroll round the school's

the marble floor and facings, copper taps and stained glass of the Roman baths that lend such splendour to the bathhouse, built at the same period as its renowned counterpart in Budapest. Other quarters of the city offer further interesting examples both of Jugendstil and historical architecture. In the Robertsau and Musau areas there are schools that look like genuine castles, while the Neudorf district teems with Jugendstil houses along the Route du Polygone and Rue Jules Rathgeber, to name but two streets.

Reflections and Translucence

In the 20th century buildings were designed not only with the way they would reflect in water in mind, but also, as glass and metal were increasingly used, to reflect their environment. Pink sandstone is still a traditional construction material, as is concrete, but new techniques have given rise to larger, looser-limbed buildings that unfold almost organically. Huge bay windows bring the outside world inside and turn buildings into temples of light at night.

There are few experiences more magical than being in the Museum of Modern and Contemporary Art and catching a glimpse of the steeples and spires of the Middle Ages rising into the sky between two paintings. There are few sights more impressive than the immense crater of light of the European Parliament in the dead of night or the utterly futuristic northern tram terminus at Hoenheim.

Additional showpieces of recent architectural achievement are university campuses. Strasbourg has some 50,000 students and 5,000 researchers at the Marc Bloch, Robert Schuman and Louis Pasteur Universities and its exclusive *grandes écoles*. One of Louis Pasteur University's most eminent members is Professor Jean-Marie Lehn, who won the Nobel Prize for Chemistry in 1987. He was behind the construction of the Institute of Science and Supramolecular Engineering

superb garden. There they can admire the multicoloured fresco on its ceramic facade, decorated with women's faces in style reminiscent of Mucha's posters.

Not far away rises the great bulk of the municipal bathhouse. Its red, fortress-like facade, ringed with a circular pathway, gives no hint of the wonders inside. The entrance is topped by a round cupola. Going past the wooden ticket office you find yourself at the head of a staircase that takes you down into 1900, into a world given over to the joys of bathing, of the Turkish bath and sauna. The sea is the inspiration behind the sumptuous tubs and frescoes of the large and small baths. But it is

(ISIS). It was built on the Esplanade, military land that was repurposed in the 1970s to become part residential area, part university campus. The tall blue shape of ISIS offers a harmonious counterpoint to the low sweep of the Law Faculty. Among the most remarkable contemporary constructions are the boldly translucent buildings that house the Innovation Research Pole (API) and the International Space University (ISU) in the research and business park of Illkirch-Graffenstaden. There universities, laboratories and companies work side-by-side. Strasbourg's universities and *grandes écoles* draw ever growing numbers of students and some older buildings have been converted into lodgings for them. One such building is the Commanderie Saint-Jean (the former residence of the commander of the knights of Saint John) in the Petite France district, which has been attributed to students at the civil servants' *grande école*, ENA. Its old gatehouse has a *trompe l'œil* wall reminiscent of the technical tricks of Renaissance painters. Every care has been taken to preserve the integrity of the Commanderie, a key part of the Petite France landscape. The only concession to modernity has been the addition of an auditorium built on the outside. Again great care was taken to ensure it blends with the surroundings.

This painstaking effort to craft a fine balance between old and new is again reflected in the European Management and Economy Pole, a business school which has been housed in the old military ordnance building on the Boulevard d'Anvers. The flow of students in and out of the red brick building adds to the bustle of one of the city's busiest markets on the square outside the building. It is a typical snapshot of a city where academia is part and parcel of everyday life.

Many of the new architectural projects focus on the city gate, an old dock area built in the 19th century. A building that will house the new contemporary archives library is under construction there. It will be followed by a music and dance centre and an extensive multimedia library.

Designed to rise like a figurehead on the dockfront of the Port d'Austerlitz, the library will be housed in a repurposed munitions depot, part of the city's industrial heritage dating back to the 1930s. It will be rebuilt and enlarged so as to offer a user-friendly facility that brings books and reading to life. The focal point of Strasbourg City Council's library network, it will boast an exceptionally rich collection of European literature and rare books, while also giving illustration and music pride of place.

Both the contemporary archives and the new library will be built into a new district where footbridges will cross the old docks. Water was the original raison d'être of the docks and that will be regularly celebrated: there will be a marina and *guingettes* (popular dances traditionally held by the waterside).

2

Subterranean City

"Cities always remind me of those tombs where the accumulated wealth of the dead was stored."
Julien Green

Above: *Deep in its bowels, an old granary known as
the "Cornucopia" shelters the remains of a Roman wall.*
Page right, top to bottom: *The stela depicting four gods discovered on
Place Kléber. The side depicting Juno, from the 3rd century AD,
and the funerary portrait of a man, which goes back to the 2nd century AD.*

It is from the upper deck of a bus or slipping through the night on a translucent tram that we are afforded the best vantage points into the life that goes on behind Strasbourg's closed doors. A curtain lifts, a light comes on, and we enter for a moment an unknown interior. A Christmas tree, a Hanukkah lamp, a cake hot out of the oven, a young man at his computer, a cat, the pendant of a chandelier, the corner of a bookshelf – all glimpses of early 21st century life.

But the secret life of the Strasbourg of yore also lies below the ground, haunted by the ghosts of the dead city. Several invisible cities live on in memory.

The most ancient is the Roman city, pieces of which are unearthed by every new building project. The most mysterious is the city of legend with its subterranean lake below the cathedral and the secret passages that twist and turn beneath today's streets. Nor should we forget wartime Strasbourg whose military engineering remains riddle the earth. But the bowels of the city are not inhabited solely by the sepulchral shadows of the past. They are put to the cheery uses of the present – as wine cellars and theatre venues.

One thing has not changed over the centuries, however. It is the groundwater that lies between two and eight metres down and has remained to this day the master of all ceremonies. The wooden pillars which have held the foundations of the cathedral stable for hundreds of years are lapped by the same waters as the buildings of today.

Roman all over the place

Standing a little apart on the Place Broglie behind the opera house is a long, low, heavily ribbed, freestone building which has caught the eye since it was repurposed to house the National Rhine Opera's workshops and rehearsal rooms. When it was built in 1441, it was known as the Kornspeicher, or corn loft,

and was the city's granary in the event of food shortages or sieges.

Renovation work revealed that part of the Kornspeicher's foundations rested on the walls of the roman military camp which had been regularly strengthened to improve defences. A small 4th century section of the wall has been left uncovered in the basement of the building, as Strasbourg has no visible ground level roman remains like Cologne or Augst. The thermal baths have long vanished but the ground is crammed with earthenware pipes that once carried water. Water was supplied by an aqueduct that ran the twenty-eight kilometres from Kuttolsheim to Strasbourg. The city's archaeological museum – one of the richest in France – provides a comprehensive overview of the roman presence in Alsace.

Although it also offers exhibits from other times, it nevertheless gives pride of place to Argentoratum, the seat of the military authority and supply base for the roman camps in advanced positions on the Danube front.

The museum features a reconstituted gallo-roman house. Complete with frescoes, ordinary domestic items, roofing and hypocaust (underground heating system), it affords visitors a glimpse of everyday life at the time. Another room is devoted to the Eighth Roman Legion –the Alsatian legion *par excellence*, since it arrived in the region around 80 BC and remain billeted there until the fall of the Empire.

Several other rooms are given over to roman deities like Juno, of whom there is a fine sculpture on the stela depicting four gods that was dug up at the Place Kléber. Also on display are local celtic gods like Father Rhine, an altar to whom was unearthed in Rue du Puits. Special treatment is given to the shrine of Mithra the sun god, worship of whom rivalled nascent Christianity. Although only a few fragments of the work remained, they have been pieced together in a polychrome mould that reconstitutes an entire relief devoted to the persian sun god.

As digs have advanced, they have revealed that civilian settlements living alongside the army encampments were far more numerous than originally thought. There may have been as many as three times more people living outside the camp than within, which lends added credence to the view that the town was economically vibrant. Many domestic utensils, from rudimentary pottery to sigillated ceramics, as well as amphorae for importing spanish and italian wine, olive oil, atlantic oysters and salted meat and fish have been found. They provide valuable clues to the diet and customs of the time and add to the international sum of archaeological knowledge.

Recent digs

The topography of ancient times is recognisable in the city of today. In recent years civil engineering projects, like the laying of the tramway system have deepened knowledge, helping to refine understanding of water systems, trench digging and successive additions to settlement walls – in a word, how the founders of Argentoratum and their successors mastered the environment to extend the city and organise its economy and defense. New finds continue to surprise and delight archaeologists on their digs. Recently numerous private houses were unearthed on Place de l'Homme de Fer and Rue de la Mésange.

One surprising find – as the people of Strasbourg who have explored the many digs open to the public have seen for themselves – was a set of dwellings thought to date back to the 1st or 2nd century. Even wooden parts like walls and floors were in remarkable condition thanks to the perfectly balanced moisture levels in Strasbourg's peaty earth. The community appears to have been structured much along the lines of the one that thrived in the Grand-Rue with its ironsmiths, bronzesmiths, carpenters and other tradesmen who worked in the service of the army.

De profundis

Nobody had so much as suspected the existence of another major discovery – that of a necropolis dating from the Early Middle Ages, between the 8th and 10th centuries. Its score of tombs make it the largest necropolis ever discovered on Strasbourg's islands. It was unearthed 1.3 metres below the roadway on the Place Broglie, near the Bank of France. It is contemporary with the founding of the parishes of Saint-Thomas's Cathedral and the Convent of Saint-Etienne. The ground below Saint-Etienne contains the remains of part of a basilica built in the 5th century – a time of transition when the Romans were to be forced out of Alsace by the Huns.

There is, however, little trace of the various edifices that succeeded each other over time on the spot where the cathedral now stands. The only exception are the foliate and historiated capitals and carved ornaments which testify to the existence of the eastern end of the crypt of the basilica built by Bishop Wernher in 1015.

That was also the time of the legend of the underground lake as told by Alsatian story-teller and folk historian Jean Variot in his work *l'Alsace éternelle* in 1929.

"They had to dig deep to lay the foundations of the vast edifice they had planned. First they encountered quicksand, then the waters of an underground lake. They did not want to go on digging at this location, but Bishop Wernher was anxious to see the building erected on the very place where the first Christians had prayed. The piles had to be driven deep and a gigantic effort, which did honour to the ingenuity and patience of men, had to be furnished. The foundations, unique in the world, were completed only in the year that Bishop Wernher yielded up his soul to God, which was in 1028. Thereafter, many a person claimed to have heard the lapping of the waters of a subterranean lake. Late at night, when the city is deserted, the same people said they sometimes heard the sound of oars stroking the water. The entrance to the tunnel that led down to the lake was in the cellar of the house that stood next to the Cerf pharmacy, opposite the cathedral. One day several centuries ago, a certain group of students and burghers equipped with ropes, picks, shovels and lanterns entered the cellar but recoiled on hearing noises that rose up towards them. They were human groans or the cries of larvae and animals unknown. Some even asserted that when they peered into the abyss, they saw terrifying faces which breathed poison. They blocked the hole leading to the abyss with boulders and rubble."

The historical cellars of the Hospices de Strasbourg

Although underground reaches have always fired the imagination, they always have some basis in specific historical fact. Strasbourg, for example, can justifiably claim to be the first city to have authorised the dissection of corpses. The first autopsy took place in 1517, fifty years before the Faculty of Paris secured permission. It was carried out on a gallows victim whose body was handed over to city surgeons by the magistrate and led to anatomical drawings published by the printer Johan Schott.

The legend of the underground lake below the cathedral goes back to the Middle Ages. This engraving shows the well in the southern aisle that led down to it.

The hospital's Saint-Erhardt chapel that had fallen into disuse under the Reform was subsequently used as an autopsy theatre from 1670 to 1875 as the inscription *Theatrum anatomicum* on its facade testifies. There was a rumour that an opening in the side wall of the chapel was used to slip hung or drowned corpses down into the cellar so that the medical students could ply their dastardly trade.

The chapel's vaults were part of a formidable labyrinth of underground passages that communicated with cellars dating back to medieval times which had survived a fire and modifications to the burghers' hospital built in 1398. The cellars contained casks of wine that boasted magnificently sculpted braces. The wine was a 1472 vintage and was served to distinguished guests. These included representatives of the people of Zurich come to testify to the support they had demonstrated in 1576 or, much closer to us, General Leclerc, who was offered a glass on liberating Strasbourg in 1944. He was the last visitor to sample the vintage, which was always replaced by the same quantity of the wine of the year.

In the old days many of the town's burghers spent a peaceful old age in the hospital which they had chosen as their place of retirement. As a charity, it lived and grew wealthy on the many legacies willed to it to meet its needs. The quality of the food and wine served were the equal of the best cuisine to be found anywhere. Even today the wines, that can be bought at the historic cellars of the Hospices de Strasbourg, perpetuate its reputation of yore.

Ashes to ashes

The statue of the Strasbourgeois General Kléber rises haughtily in the centre of the square that bears his name, Place Kléber. He holds an ultimatum from Lord Keith, admiral of the British navy, demanding the surrender of the troops under his command in Egypt in 1800 at the time of revolutionary wars. Kléber's answer was to the point: "Soldiers, our reply to a letter of such insolence will be victory. Prepare to fight."

But the victor of the battle of Heliopolis only had time to set out on his reconquest of the Middle East, because on 14th June, 1800, he was assassinated in Cairo shortly after retaking it. On 14th June, 1840, Strasbourg unveiled Philipe Grass's statue of the general which had arrived in the city by boat along the Rhône-to-Rhine Canal and passed through the lock of the Ponts Couverts.

The statue is now a familiar feature of the square. People come and go without realising that it is also a mausoleum : beneath the statue are the general's remains, save for his embalmed heart that rests in Paris in the crypt of the Invalides.

Jean Baptiste Kléber was born in Strasbourg in 1753. He began his career as an architect and several monuments in Belfort and Thann in eastern France are his work. His career in the army was an eventful one that came to a violent end in Egypt. Even after his death, his coffin experienced trials and tribulations before finally coming home to Strasbourg.

In July 1801 his troops took his remains with them when they pulled out of Egypt. It was a moving journey : his coffin was taken on-board a ship at Rosette and descended the Nile under the guard of the grenadiers. He was temporarily buried in a chapel of the Château d'If in Marseilles until 7th September, 1818, when the coffin was transferred to Strasbourg in a carriage drawn by six horses with black-ribboned drums, while buglers played a funereal march. On arriving in Strasbourg his body was taken straight to the cathedral to the tolling of all the city's bells. His resting place was for a long time the chapel of Saint-Laurent, as political changes constantly led to the postponement of a monument erected in his honour. It was only on the 40th anniversary of his death that a memorable ceremony inaugurated his tomb.

Formidable fort

At Wolfisheim an extremely well preserved fort, originally called Fort Bismarck, now bears General Kléber's name. It is part of a fortified defence ring built in 1872 by General von Moltke, after France ceded Alsace-Lorraine to Prussia. Visitors can tour the twelve forts by following a cycling and walking route that is currently being finalised. There were in fact two rings : one surrounded Strasbourg, while the second was ten kilometres further out and afforded protection to the different towns around Strasbourg. The War Gate – the Porte de la Guerre, or Kriegsthor – stands to the west of the city in the Glacis Park. Its sheer size and near-perfect state of preservation are impressive indeed. It is built from freestone and boasts two monumental entrances designed for military vehicles to pass through and for the evacuation of people in the event of a siege. The War Gate is part of an enormous fortification scheme that comprises several small forts. As all such military constructions had been dismantled in Germany under the terms of the Treaty of Versailles, this defensive system is now the only one of its kind still standing. A twelve metres high compacted earth mound housed a warren of tunnels leading to the munitions store, exercise rooms, dormitories and supplies and equipment stores. To strengthen defences, a moat was especially dug. Called the Fossé des Remparts, water from the Rivers Ill and Bruche flowed into it. A sluice gate buried beneath the communication line held water in the moat, which is now home to ducks, swans and otters.

Strollers enjoying a walk in the area with its many gardens forget its original vocation. They blithely take a seat on an armour-plated casemate caponniere without thinking that its narrow loopholes were once designed for cannon fire.

The City of Strasbourg recently acquired the fortification which is to have a new calling at the service of the arts and culture. Artists have already set up workshops and studios in some of the forts.

Drained of colour

Another out-of-the-ordinary journey to the hidden heart of the city is one to its sewerage system, also engineered in the late 19th century. By 1880 Strasbourg already boasted twenty-two kilometres of drains. Much water will have flowed through them by the time the upgrading work on the wastewater treatment plant at Wantzenau this year makes it a model of technical performance and sustainable development.

One of the simplest paths to take through Strasbourg's sewers is to follow the old Fossé des Tanneurs – the Tanners' Trench. It runs from the River Ill in Place Benjamin Zix, along Rue du Fossé des Tanneurs, Rue de la Haute Montée, Rue de la Mésange and Place Broglie, and on into the Faux Rempart Canal behind the theatre. Work to cover the drainage system began in 1828 but today's sewers follow the same route below ground.

The light down under is bluish and the air damp and misty. A stench assail you. The only sound that breaks the silence in these lower depths is that of feet wading through the brown, clammy water. The old tunnels have been remarkably constructed with their non-porous brick facing and polished sandstone conduits. The most recent additions are concrete. At regular intervals the collectors – long angled bends carved into the stone or just plain holes – pour wastewater from buildings and streets into the system.

The collectors all bear nameplates so that visitors can get their bearings in relation to landmarks above ground like the Aubette concert hall, City Hall and other stages on the gently sloping sewer circuit. As the National Theatre near the Place Broglie draws closer the tunnels get higher and wider. There are even footpaths on either side of the slimy sewerage.

Above: *Under the Place Broglie a journey to the centre of the sewers.*
Page right: *The cellars of the Hospices de Strasbourg are the*
storehouses of heady potions that have lost none of their special virtues.

Above: *Below the Palais Universitaire the hoplites
of the Temple of Aphaia in Aegina wage their last shadow combat.*
Page right: *In the light of day peace reigns over the old
fortifications. The Citadelle is popular with strollers,
while the Glacis Fort now houses artists' studios.*

Eventually the tunnels open out into a space that is wide enough for a boat. Hardly, surprising, therefore, that directors have used it as a setting for films. You leave the sewers by stepping out through a door, kept otherwise locked, and on to the banks of the Ill to revel in the fresh air, daylight and green grass that grows on the edge of the Faux Rempart Canal.

Subterranean songs

It was in 1872, when Strasbourg belonged to Germany, that Professor Michaelis, director of the Institute of Classical Archaeology, began collecting plaster-cast reproductions of Greek sculptures. The Palais Universitaire has 350 in underground storage.

The moulds are made in workshops in Berlin, Athens, Dresden, London, Paris, Rome and Vienna and belong to a long lineage that traces the history of greek sculpture from its Middle Eastern roots down to its roman legacy. They were initially on the first storey, whose backdrop of vividly painted Pompei red brought colours into their own.

Greek statuary is not what you would usually expect to find underground. Much more fitting is public transport. The underground tramway station draws thousands of commuters and tourists daily into the bowels of the city. Over 35,000 commuters pass through it, three-quarters of whom use regional express trains. Of all Strasbourg's stations it is the only one to lie seventeen metres below ground, where there is no change of season. The same green light bathes the station day in day out, but it is not a sickly hue.

New York artist, Barbara Kruger, has scattered little messages on the eleven steps leading down into the station, on the platforms, on the concrete beams and walls. But what really catches the eye is the giant screen print depicting a padlocked head which proclaims "Empathy can change the world".

Greater scrutiny, however, is needed to decipher the twelve triptychs embedded in the ground. They are little treasures of word and image that proffer such pieces of advice as "Take the time to live", "Smile at your neighbour" and "Put things in perspective". They are designed to give commuters food for thought before they get into the carriage. A pre-recorded loud-speaker system using a distinctive variety of accents and voices gives the impression that it is speaking to you and you alone as it announces, "This stop is Strasbourg Train Station".

Strasbourg's many cultural and entertainment venues draw pleasure-seekers in their thousands into the city's underground for outings at places such as Taps Scala, an old cinema at Neudorf that has been converted into a theatre. There is also the Boîte Noire (Black Box) theatre, the exhibition hall in the Chamber of Commerce and Industry and the Odyssée, a marvellous cinema built in 1913. Not to mention the cellar restaurants that hum with post-show conversations down in the depths of the city where one of the walls belongs to times that are gone but not forgotten!

3

Pink Shadow

When he was five years old Gustave Doré would leave his home in the Rue des Ecrivains and head for the Place de la Cathédrale (Cathedral Square) where his tutor, Monsieur Vergnette, awaited him. The hands of the great clock told him the time, while grimacing gargoyles peered down at the tiny figure engulfed in the vast shadows of the cathedral. When he left Strasbourg six years later, the towering structure pocked with light and crawling with spider-like sculptures had been already indelibly etched on his imagination since childhood. He had grown up in the shadow of the cathedral and the statuary of Erwin de Steinbach and his daughter, Sabine, was already part of the phantasmagoric world that he would express in his illustrations.

Every day, like Gustave Doré with his child's eyes, people from outside town experience the thrill of glimpsing the cathedral for the first time. Even Strasbourg's inhabitants remain enthralled. They cannot escape the wonder of the cathedral and, were they to try, they would find themselves irresistibly drawn back.

Visitors emerging from the Rue des Hallebardes have their "breath taken away", to quote art critic Mario Praz, by the sight before them, which he describes thus: "Rigid stone lacework rises abruptly like a rock face. One is seized by a sense of vertigo at its height and one feels drawn upwards all the more powerfully for there being but one spire. It is the Mount Cervin of cathedrals."

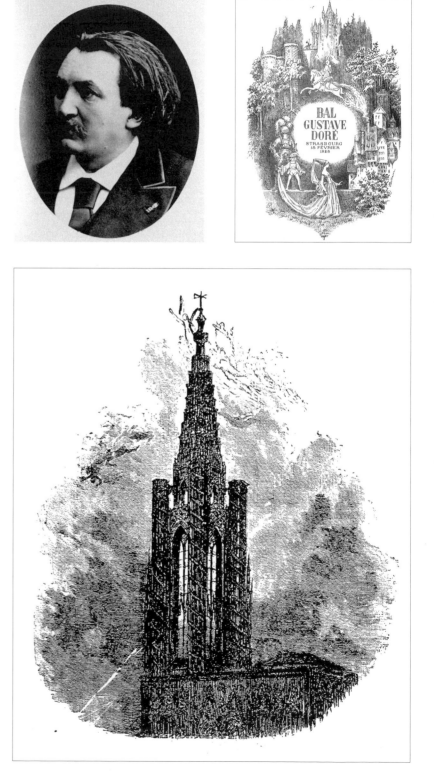

Page left: *Gustave Doré's* Entre Ciel et Terre *(Between Heaven and Earth), 1862, oil on canvas.*
Facing: *Portrait of the artist and his engravings.*

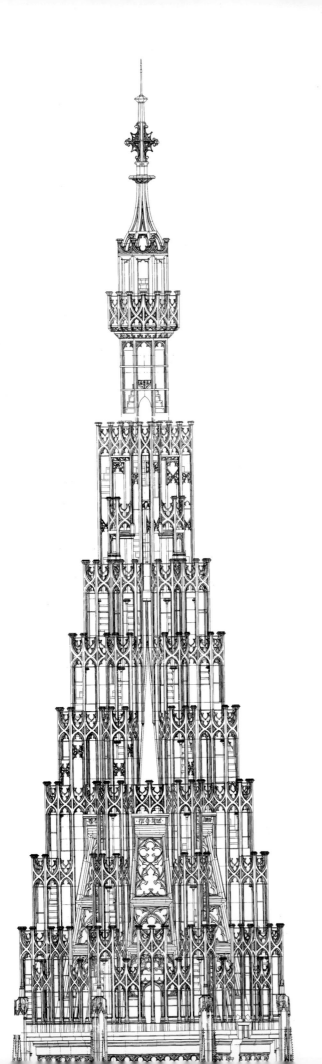

Four Centuries of Construction

A little to one side on the nearby Place du Château stands the Museum Oeuvre Notre-Dame, whose second story features a bust of Nicolas Gerhaert de Leyde. It is a self-portrait of this sculptor of genius who arrived from the Netherlands in the mid-15th century. He was behind one of the cathedral's prettiest smiles, that of the Madonna and Child from the Busnang epitaph in Saint John's Chapel.

The museum's windows look out onto the nave that stretches like a vast ship from the transept tower overlooking the chancel to the single spire atop the great west facade. Each stage in the building of the cathedral can be read chronologically from east to west. Bishop Werner of the Habsbourg dynasty began building in 1015, but his basilica was damaged by a succession of fires. In 1176 reconstruction began on the north transept that can still be seen today. Construction of the nave commenced in the mid-13th century. It was a long slow process that was eventually completed in 1277 when Bishop Conrad de Lichtenberg laid the first stone of the facade. A succession of master builders worked on the facade until it was finally completed in 1439. The parchments on which Erwin de Steinbach, Michel de Fribourg,

Ulrich d'Ensingen and Jean Hulz de Cologne drew up their plans have been preserved to this day, an almost unheard-of stroke of luck.

The blueprint attributed to Hans Hammer before 1490 describes a twin-towered cathedral. It was never to be, however, since Strasbourg, like other cathedrals in Rhineland, has only ever had a single spire. Nevertheless, the idea of a symmetrical edifice long exercised its attraction, as the drawings by the 19th century Berlin architect, Schinkel, testify.

The Dawn of Art

Inside the cathedral's south transept a bust, made at the same time as that of Nicolas Gerhaert de Leyde, leans on the balustrade of the *cantoria*, the small choir's gallery opposite the Pilier des Anges (Angels' Column). It is sometimes called the Scrutiniser because the gaze it casts on the Angels' Column is so piercing. Of the many architects and master craftsmen involved in building the cathedral, and of whom little is often known, he is one of those of whom we know the most. His name is Hans Hammer and the many marvels of which he is the creator include the cathedral pulpit with its numerous carved sandstone and alabaster figures and its curlicue, palm-leaf and vine-branch trimmings. The carvings also depict a little dog that belonged to Geiler de Kaysersberg, the preacher for whom the pulpit was especially erected in 1485. His sermons, which drew enthusiastic crowds, would sometimes last for three hours at a time. The little dog, faithful companion of the great humanist, would doze at his feet. It was a homely detail that Hans Hammer sought to immortalise in stone on the edge of the staircase that leads up to the pulpit.

As mentioned, the bust of Hans Hammer has its gaze riveted on the Angels' Column. Its slightly dubious expression could quite possibly be to do with the legend surrounding it. The story goes like this.

When a team of master craftsmen came from Paris to bring Gothic art to the old Roman basilica of Strasbourg a strange little man was there to watch them start work. He spared them no sarcasm as he came daily to watch the Pilier des Anges gradually take shape. The column, which depicts the Last Judgement, comprises three registers of carvings that seem to spring from the main trunk of the stone column. More than the apostles or Christ surrounded by angels bearing the instruments of his Passion, it is the sheer grace of the musician angels that arouses admiration.

The great Romantic historian, Michelet, wrote that a tangible yet invisible breath of music seemed to pervade the cathedral. It does indeed seem uncluttered, full of air and light. So light, sneered the strange little man, that one wonders how it will manage to hold up the massive, heavy vault of the cathedral? The architect of the time lost patience and decided to punish the weird dimminutive sceptic by turning him to stone. He was Hans Hammer, now doomed to stare at the column until Kingdom come.

45

The men who sculpted the Angels' Column also carved the column figures, Church and Synagogue, on the facade over the south transept portal. Their work moved another great French historian, Hippolyte Taine, to say that the statues ushered in the dawn of art.

Swallows' Nests

Over the centuries opinions of Strasbourg Cathedral have changed as tastes and aesthetic canons changed. With the end of the Middle Ages came a period that disregarded gothic architecture, disdaining it as barbarian. Spare, hieratical columns and capitals flourished during the Renaissance, while festoons and curlicues were discarded. Luxuriant Spätgothik decoration, epitomised by the pulpit and font, that has visitors flocking to the cathedral today, held no attraction.

Among the pioneers of the rediscovery of the gothic art was the young Goethe. By the time he was twenty-one he was smitten with the cathedral and his first published piece, devoted to the art of German architecture, was a magnificent paean to Strasbourg Cathedral whose harmony entranced him.

The resurgence of an art that had for so long been despised was an opportunity for the architect Jean-Laurent Goetz to use the neo-gothic style to build the cathedral's lateral outer aisles in 1775. What was the purpose of this 18th century adjunct? To hide the so-called "little shops" that had sprung up along the cathedral's flanks. Upholsterers, wedding and funeral wreath flower sellers and other tradespeople peddled their wares. Some sold aqua vita and cheese, while behind other shopfronts the "cathedral swallows" plied their trade. They were women of easy virtue whose brisk business was understandably thought out of place.

Because these trades were as old as the cathedral itself and difficult to stamp out it was decided to hide them from public view by building lateral aisles. The style that once again gave gothic art pride of place prompted much criticism from members of the city's governing council. One anecdote has it that Jean-Laurent Goetz used one of the most vocal critics as a model for the gargoyles!

Page left: *The Angels' Column opposite the Astronomic Clock sounds the knell of the Last Judgement.*
Above: *The statuary depicting the figures of Synagogue (left) and Church (right) on the southern gate of the cathedral's transept are among the finest examples of french gothic sculpture. The originals are to be seen in the Museum of Œuvre-Notre-Dame, as are those of the Seducer and the Foolish Virgins (centre).*

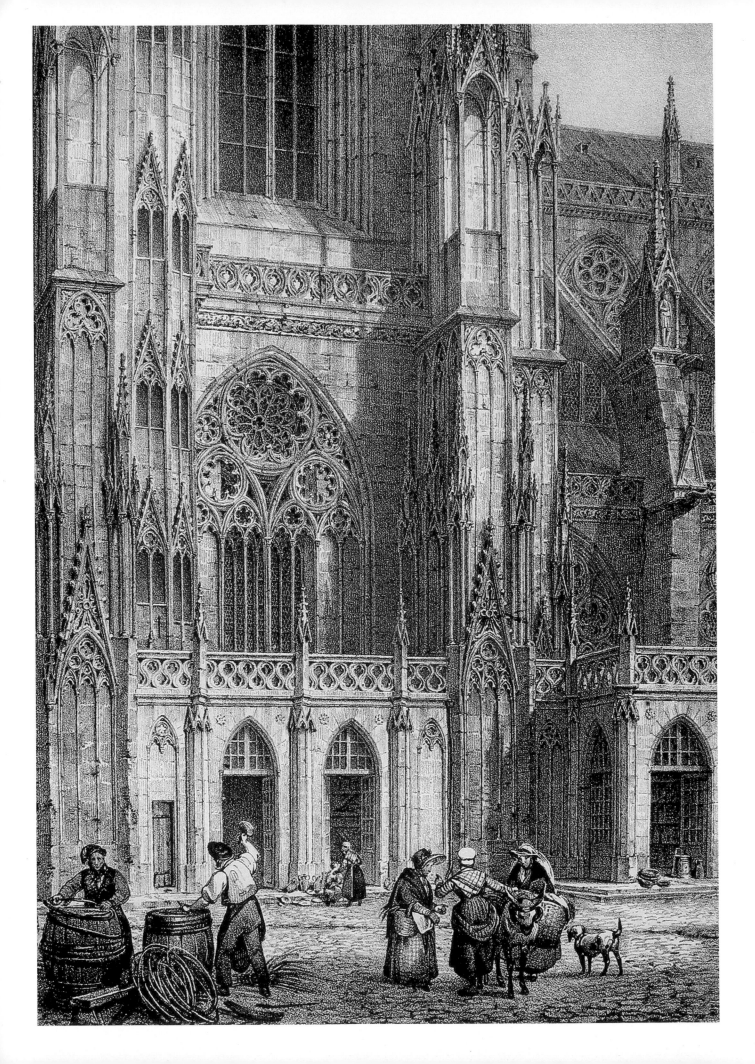

Madeleine's Skirt

The various episodes recounted above come down to us in part from the archives of the Œuvre Notre-Dame (Our Lady's Work). Initially this institution was tasked with collecting funds to build the cathedral and bringing together a team of builders and craftsmen. From then on the cathedral and the Œuvre Notre-Dame were inseparably linked. The bishop originally administered the Œuvre and building work, but at the end of the 13th century the city magistrate took over. The whole enterprise might seem on too vast a scale for a city of barely 10,000. But the religious faith and enthusiasm of the inhabitants who watched the stone miracle gradually rising towards the heavens swept to one side all obstacles. Donations poured in. A three hundred and sixty-eight pages parchment recorded all those made between 1262 and 1520.

The richest burghers gave land, vineyards, and even forests. Those who were less well-off donated casks of wine or sacks of wheat. Some local ladies had no hesitation in parting with their finery. One was the patrician Anna Blankelin who gave away her fur-lined cloak. But the most moving story is probably that of Madeleine – nothing else is known about her apart from her Christian name and that she was a servant. She sacrificed her favourite red skirt to the greater glory of the edification of Notre-Dame of Strasbourg. There were many more like her who will remain forever nameless. Their flesh and blood is as much part of the monumental edifice as its stone.

The Highest Café in the City

"Hitt grattle mer bi Wind und Sturm uff d'Schnecke nuff vum Müenschterdurm" – "Today, come rain or shine, we will climb the cathedral's towers" runs one of the Mathhis Brothers' most famous poems. These inseparable twins, born four years after the Prussian siege of 1870, have expressed better than anyone the spirit of a city of which they knew all the nooks and crannies. In the early 1900s these bachelor brothers devoted all their love to old city quarters such as Petite France and Krutenau and their inhabitants. Their dialect poems climbed the cathedral spire like many others before them. These included Goethe, Victor Hugo and Stendhal, who have recounted the ascent in gripping terms.

From the 18th century to the time of the Matthis twins a platform on the cathedral's roof housed a restaurant. It was as popular a place for a Sunday stroll as the public parks or along city ramparts. Goethe would go up there with his friends such as Lenz and Herder as dusk gathered: "Let us take ourselves up there in mid-air to the high, wide platform of the cathedral as if we still lived in the time when, as youthful companions, we would arrange to meet in the evenings in order to salute, glass in hand, the setting sun. Up there, all conversation would fade into contemplation of the country before us."

Other less well-known strollers were as taken by the quality of the beer as the grandeur of the cathedral. In the visitors book that recorded impressions of the platform from the 19th century Barbier de Thionville wrote: "In this place I savoured a jug of excellent beer." Officers from the dragoons asserted that they had climbed to the roof of the cathedral not out of curiosity but to empty a glass of beer in a café three hundred feet in the air.

Perpendicular Journey

After a certain Monsieur Pouillard who sold cheese, the name of Victor Hugo appears on the register. Other famous names from 19th century literary France follow: Vigny, Michelet, Lamartine, Musset, Heine, Tocqueville, Alexandre Dumas, Balzac, Georges Sand, Eugène Sue, and the Erckmann half of the novel writing duo

Erckmann-Chatrian. In 1838 Stendhal, Gérard de Nerval, Alexandre Dumas, Victor Hugo and Juliette Drouet could quite easily have been in Strasbourg at about the same time. Their frock coats and crinoline dress must have brushed against the winding steps and the walls of the narrow stair-tower as they made the ascent to the platform for what was literally a summit meeting. Not quite, however.

The highest point of Strasbourg Cathedral is at the very tip of its spire. It is the only cathedral to have a spiral staircase so designed and built that it goes to the very top. And although there are countless visitors to the platform far fewer dare go all the way to the spire's pinnacle. Victor Hugo used to limit his "perpendicular journey" to the platform. He nevertheless describes with great precision the final stages of the ascent that Goethe used to undertake as part of a deliberate effort to overcome his fear of heights: "Danger could begin at the very point where I stopped, from where the spire proper rises. Four open-work spiral staircases,

wrapped in a delicately tapered and crafted stone webbing, lean against the spire whose angle they follow as they creep up to what is known as the crown, some thirty feet from the lantern topped by a cross which marks the summit of the steeple. The steps are high and narrow, and become narrower the higher one climbs."

It is easy to understand why Gaston Bachelard was to say of the climb he made when he was twenty: "Ascending to and descending from absolute vertigo twice in only a few minutes marks the psyche for life. In all my nightmares I fall on to the roofs of Strasbourg."

Above: *The platform on the cathedral's roof was a much favoured place to meet up to the mid-19th century.*
Page right: *The dizzying view over the rooftops of old Strasbourg which so bewitched Victor Hugo.*

Above: *The gothic garden, or "heaven", of the Museum
of Œuvre-Notre-Dame was planted in accordance with the rules
set out by Albert the Great. It contains vegetable patches, medicinal
plants and ornamental flower beds.*
Page right: *In every nook and cranny of the edifice grotesque figures
vye for the eye of passers-by.*

Scaling the giddy heights to the very top of the spire's pinnacle is now banned because the pink sandstone has become friable. For the general public the climb has to be experienced in literature – in Goethe's memoirs or Stendhal's correspondence. Only aerial experts such as restorers are allowed up to the giddy heights.

The Cathedral Builders

Aerial experts include the *compagnons* (term given to a fraternity of master builders) of Œuvre Notre-Dame, which together with France's Historical Monuments' Department and the City of Strasbourg has carried out restoration work on the cathedral. It now is centuries-old, the only institution of its kind to have survived to present times. After escaping the turbulence of the French Revolution by the skin of its teeth, its existence was confirmed by the Consular decree of 3rd Frimaire (month of sleet) in Year XII of the Revolution. In the wake of the Franco-Prussian War of 1870 it restored the damaged cathedral. Between 1907 and 1923 it helped to consolidate the foundations and later repaired the crossing tower damaged by the bombing in 1944.

Its restoration team comprises some forty carvers, sculptors and other specialised craftsmen. They perpetuate the age-old skills of their forebears by working with the hand-held tools of the Middle Ages – an array of hammers, mallets and chisels – as well as the technology of today.

The cathedral spire is currently undergoing renovation. The Œuvre Notre-Dame conducted a stone-by-stone examination to assess wear and tear and identify repair needs. The head architect of the Historical Monuments Service then carried out analyses and conservation work began. Restorers and stonecutters can be seen at work in a vast workshop on the Plaine des Bouchers. On entering, huge blocks of sandstone tell visitors they are in a place dedicated to preserving the cathedral. Stone is not the only material being worked on. There is a forge where the metal doorway frames are repaired. A carpentry workshop and a plaster-casting workshop also complement the work of the stone carvers and sculptors who shape the statuary that adorns the cathedral. In the courtyard railings, pinnacles, turrets and delicately indented staircases are ready and waiting to be put in place on the spire. For not only do the *compagnons* possess the skills of master craftsmen, they are also high-wire walkers with no fear of heights.

The spire will soon shed its hood of scaffolding, but more renovation work is already scheduled because there is no such thing as a finished cathedral.

Œuvre Notre-Dame: a dream museum

Sculptors and stonecutters used to work in the twinned medieval and renaissance buildings on the Place du Château that are home to the museum of Œuvre Notre-Dame. In 1931 section containing their workshops was converted into the museum which is devoted to the art of the Rhineland from its origins to the 17th century. It is here that the cathedral's most famous original statues are exhibited.

The museum exudes an irresistible charm. Each room has its own special atmosphere. Some are dark

The great Romantic historian, Michelet, wrote that an invisible, yet tangible, strain of music seemed to pervade the cathedral.

Page left, above: *craftsman from Œuvre Notre-Dame at work. Rough sketches of sculptures from Strasbourg Cathedral by Eugene Delacroix in 1855.*
Page left, below, left: Saint Catherine and Saint Madeleine, *15th century painting on wood by K. Witz.*
Below, right: Corbeille de verres *(glasses in a basket), painted by S. Stoskopff in 1644.*

but shimmering with subdued light from stained glass windows, while the panelling in others creates a cosy feel. The former stonecutters' lodge is impressive with its painted ceiling and statues of the Three Wise Men bearing lavish gifts. The next room is like a nave with a ceiling that measures over ten metres high. It boasts some of the greatest masterpieces of gothic art. The original statues of Church and Synagogue stand cheek-by-jowl with the Seducer and the Wise and Foolish Virgins. Ravishingly bejewelled Virtues mincingly conquer Vices as the Prophets look on sternly from under their bushy eyebrows.

In this enclosed space visitors are in closed proximity to the centuries-old statues. In this intimate face-to-face no detail escapes the eye – from the folds of a robe to the mood of a face.

This outstanding museum also boasts many other treasures. They include a stained glass window depicting the majesty of Charlemagne, paintings like "Joseph's Doubt" and "Saint Catherine and Saint Madeleine", statuettes typical of the mystical art of the Rhineland and tapestries illustrating the life of Saint Odile. The refined lifestyles of the 16th and 17th centuries are equally well represented by collections of gold artefacts, imposing deux-corps wardrobes from Alsace and still lives by Sébastien Stoskopff. Not to be missed is "Paradise", the small Gothic garden with its medicinal plants, vegetable patches and ornaments arranged in accordance with the precepts of Albert the Great.

The museum of Œuvre Notre-Dame is one of those places to which visitors endlessly yearn to return. One such visitor was the great 19th century French painter, Eugène Delacroix, who spent days at a time there, so fascinated was he by medieval sculpture: "I throw myself on the figures of angels from the 13th and 14th centuries, on the foolish virgins and on the bas-reliefs of wild proportions but of great grace and force."

4

A History
of Emotions

*"At the first verse faces paled, at the second tears flowed, at
the last rapturous enthusiasm erupted. Dietrich, his wife, and
the young officer fell weeping into each others' arms. The
anthem of the fatherland had been found."*

Alphonse de Lamartine

A city cannot come through two thousand years of history without signs and scars to show for it. The traces of the past are everywhere in Strasbourg. Picturesque street names, for example, like Lace Street (Rue des Dentelles) or Rose Bath Street (Rue du Bain-aux-Roses), whose pure poetry springs from rough french translations of the german. The past steeps the city's architecture, whose sheer variety prompted Le Corbusier to say "one's gaze is never bored in Strasbourg". History is everywhere in details known only to the happy few, such as the incision cut into the cathedral's south face which sets the exact height authorised for the oriel windows of the half-timber houses. On a corner of the Rue du Faubourg-de-Pierre a placard bearing the signature of General Leclerc has hung since the liberation of Strasbourg in 1944. Aside from these visible signs there are places that are inhabited by the resonance of what happened there, by the intensity of individual and collective emotions. Knights once rolled in the dust and swords clanged at the jousting tournaments on a patch of land that in the 18th century became the Place Broglie, a favorite strolling place for plumed officers and *belles dames* in rustling crinoline dresses. The city's squares and *places* have always been focal points for its people at critical times in public life. Others have subsided into an anonymity revived only by the chroniclers of a history rich in emotion. Let us look at just some of the watersheds of Strasbourg's emotional past.

The Strasbourg Oaths

The scene of one of the city's earliest memories is the Plaine des Bouchers (Butchers' Plain) on the edge of the old city in what is today an industrial neighborhood like there are in so many cities. On 24th February, 842, Charlemagne's grandsons, Louis the German and Charles the Bald met there together with their armies to swear an oath of alliance against their brother Lothair. Charles spoke a romance language and Louis a germanic language. A snowstorm raged as the two brothers swore the oath in their own and each other's language. It began like this: "By God's love and by this Christian people and our common salvation, from this day forth, as far as God gives me to know and to have power, I will so aid my brother…" They were not only ones to swear the oath. Motionless in the snow and cold like an army of white ghosts, their armies, too, pledged mutual allegiance and to desert their chiefs if they foreswore the oath.

The Strasbourg Oaths were but one episode in a war of succession. They have come down to us thanks to one man – Nithard, the natural son of Charlemagne who was also one of Charles the Bald's much-valued

Vor Stellung des Jährlichen Schwörtags.

advisors. By writing down his account of the oaths he bequeathed to posterity the oldest written text in vernacular French.

The following year at Verdun the three brothers, Charles, Louis and Lothair, met to sign the treaty that gave Louis the kingdom of the East Franks (Germany) and Charles that of the West Franks (France). Lothair got the middle kingdom which included Alsace. Stretching from the North Sea to the Mediterranean, it was called Lotharingia. It was an unstable kingdom, however, and lasted only twenty-seven years. In 870 Alsace became part of the East Frankish kingdom of Louis the German under the terms of a treaty signed at Meersen. When Otto the Great brought together the Germanic territories in the Holy Roman Empire in 962, Strasbourg was incorporated as an independent republic. Its future had been mapped out for the next eight centuries.

The Schwoertag

Another time, another place. The time was the flourishing 14th century and the place was the cathedral, though long before the spire was completed in 1439. The day was a Tuesday – it had to be a Tuesday – at the beginning of January. The people of Strasbourg had barely got over the festivities in the wake of the swearing-in of their new Ammeister. Since the city had become a free imperial city after rising up against episcopal rule, the Ammeister represented trade and craft corporations, or guilds, within the Magistrate, the name given to the city council. The pealing of the cathedral's bells over the city issued a call to converge on Cathedral Square. A great dais bedecked in the red and white colors of the city had been erected. The day was Schwoertag, when the city's burghers aged 18 and over solemnly swore allegiance to the Constitution of

Strasbourg that had been drawn up in 1334. From all the surrounding streets processions flowed into the cathedral square with pomp and ceremony. There was not a single woman, as only men were admitted to a ceremony whose set ritual was to remain broadly unchanged until the French Revolution. As 10 o'clock struck, the reading of the constitution began. Silence fell. Not a bell, not a trumpet, not a cymbal could be heard. The hush was reverential as a sense of belonging to the city of Strasbourg imbued all the men present. On the dais surrounded by his peers, the Ammeister swore an oath of allegiance to the Constitution. He then called on the crowd assembled before him to remove their hats, raise their hands and do the same. And he ended with these words: "May God grant you prosperity, happiness, His blessings and long life." The following Sunday the Ammeister and his fellow Magistrate members would visit the guilds which the city's traders and craftsmen had formed. "Dear friends

and citizens," he would say, before going on to stress the duties and tasks that befell each corporation. It was a long day. He had to do the rounds of a score of guilds, of which the most important was the boatmen's. The boatmen held the key to the prosperity of a town that depended on the river for trade. The Ancienne Douane (Old Customs) through which merchandise from Flanders, Italy and elsewhere passed testifies to that time. The Ammeister's tour would close after dark with a torchlit procession back to the Pfalz, the old city hall on Place Saint-Martin, now Place Gutenberg.

The Reformation

The Pfalz, a Gothic building that no longer exists, was the venue for a decisive day in Strasbourg's religious history. In February 1529 the sovereign assembly of the city's burgher masters passed a motion tabled by the senate for the "abolition of Mass until

such time as it was proven that it was agreeable to God." Of the three hundred assembly members only one did not vote for abolition. Strasbourg had ceased to be a catholic city.

It was in 1518 that the people of the city first woke to find placards on the doors of the cathedral advocating the beliefs of Martin Luther. From this time onwards, the ideas of the Reform made headway thanks to the work and teachings of great humanists like Wimpheling, Sebastien Brant and Geiler de Kaysersberg. The latter, who gave sermons at the cathedral, used to deliver damning indictments of Church abuses in the late 15th century. The crowds he drew were so large that he had to switch from the chapel of Saint Laurent to the cathedral's nave. There it was in 1485 that Hans Hammer built for him the marvelous gothic pulpit that visitors can still admire today.

Geiler de Kaysersberg was succeeded in the next century by another preacher who also fired crowds with the same passion. His name was Mathieu Zell and his german-language sermons were not only denunciations of the Catholic Church, they also propounded the new ideas of the Reformation. Many of those who came to listen were young people – craftsmen and traders like carpenters, gardeners and butchers. When the episcopal authorities wrapped the pink sandstone pulpit in chains to prevent Zell from speaking, the carpenters of the Rue du Maroquin built him a portable wooden one. From there he continued to preach the good news.

The bishop made representations to the Magistrate to pressure Mathieu Zell into moderating his sermons, but to no avail. He was soon joined by other evangelists of renown like Martin Bucer. Strasbourg, which had welcomed Gutenberg in the previous century, was the cradle of a masterly new invention – the printing press. It played a powerful role in relaying the new ideas of the Reformation which were to spread like wildfire.

Strasbourg slipped smoothly into the Reformation like a hand into a glove. Martin Bucer swiftly became the leader of the Protestants. A believer in the value of education, he created the "High School" in 1538, making Jean Sturm its headmaster. In 1621 it became a university.

Strasbourg becomes French

At about the same time Alsace became one of the main battlefields in the Thirty Years' War which broke out in Bohemia in 1618 following conflict between Catholics and Protestants. It soon spread to the entire Holy Roman Empire.

Skilful negotiating saved Strasbourg from invasion by the troops of General Mansfeld who, in the service of the Protestants, looted and plundered as they went. In 1632 invading Swedish forces occupied Alsace. They were followed by French, Imperial then Spanish troops. The war was ended by the Treaty of Westphalia in 1648 which gave France the Habsburgs' possessions in Alsace. Strasbourg remained a free republic, but not for long.

When Louis XIV invaded Holland in 1672, the city allowed the Imperial troops to cross the Rhine Bridge but refused the French passage. France had no choice but to force Strasbourg to comply. It put in place a network of customs barriers to starve the city of trade. Then, in September 1681, Louvois and an army of 30,000 seized the Kehl Bridge and encircled Strasbourg demanding that it surrender on pain of being wiped out by iron and fire. The Magistrate had to give way, but only did so after securing enough time to draw up ten conditions of surrender. Subject to approval by Louvois and Louis XIV, they ensured the city's basic freedoms, allowing it to keep its constitution and religion as well as its financial and legal powers. The document is now conserved in the municipal archives, complete with the ink blotches and crossings-out that show how hurriedly it was drawn up.

Pages 64-65: *In 1681 Strasbourg surrendered to King Louis XIV's French troops. Louvois and the city authorities signed a treaty of surrender. It contained ten articles which enshrined the city's right to retain its constitution and religion.*

Nous François Michel Le Tellier marquis de Louvois Secretaire d'Estat et des
commandements de Sa Ma.té, Et Joseph de Ponts Baron de Montclar Lieutenant gnal des
armées du Roy commandant pour Sa Ma.té en Alsace, Avons en vertu du pouvoir
a nous accordé par Sa Ma.té pour recevoir la ville de Strasbourg a son obeissance,
mis les apostiz cy dessous dont nous promettons fournir la ratification de sa Ma.té
et la remettre au magistrat de Strasbourg entre cy et dix jours,

1

Le Roy
reçoit la ville
et toutes ses
dependances
en sa roy.alle
protection

La ville de Strasbourg à l'exemple de Monsieur
l'Evêque de Strasbourg, le Comte de Hanau, Seigneur
de Fleckenstein et de la Noblesse de la basse Alsace
reçonnoit Sa Majesté ~~Seigneur et~~ Tres Chrehienne pour son
Souverain ~~Protecteur~~.

2

accordé

Sa Majesté confirmera tous les anciens Privileges,
Droits, Statuts et Coutumes de la Ville de Strasbourg,
tant Ecclesiastiques que Politiques, conformement
au Traitté de Paix de Westphalie, confirmé par
celuy de Nimegue.

3

accordé pour
jouir de tout
ce qui regarde
les biens ecclesias
tiques semants
qu'il est present
par le traité de
munster a la
reserve du corps
de l'eglise de nostre
dame autrement
nommée le dôme
qui sera rendue aux catoliques

Majesté laissera le libre exercice de la
Religion comme il a été depuis l'Année 1624. jusques
à present, avec toutes les Eglises et Ecoles, et ne permettra
à qui que ce soit, d'y faire des pretensions, ny aux biens
Ecclesiastiques, Fondations et Couvents, à scavoir l'Abbaye
de St. Etienne le Bapitre de St. Thomas, St. Marc,
St. Guillaume, aux Touts Saints, et tous les autres
compris et non compris, mais les conservera à perpetuité
à la Ville et ses habitans.

1.Mrs. voudront bon neanmoins qu'ils puissent se servir
clochés de la ... esglise pour tous les usages cy devant pratiqués
hors pour sonner leurs prieres.

Against most of the condition, in the margins are Louvois's marks of approval. Nevertheless, Strasbourg was not allowed to stamp its own currency or possess its own artillery. It also had to return the cathedral to Catholicism.

Louvois and members of the Magistrate officially put their names to the terms of surrender on the afternoon of 30th September, 1681, in a farmer's house at Illkirch. The French troops immediately entered the city as its people looked on in amazement. Ten infantry battalions stationed themselves on the ramparts, while the inhabitants of Barfüsserplatz, (Franciscan Square) today the Place Kléber, watched three armoured cavalry squadrons set up barracks there.

The little republic had become overnight a "*ville libre royale*" and capital of the province of Alsace without striking a blow. Louvois sent a dispatch to Louis XIV – "Sire, Strasbourg is yours" – and the king set out. He arrived in Strasbourg with his royal train on 23rd October to the deafening sound of the last salvoes the Strasbourg artillery was to fire from the cannon slits in the battlements.

In honor of Louis XV

Some sixty years later there was a very different atmosphere in the city when it celebrated a visit from Louis XV between 5th and 10th October, 1744. Instead of the chilly watchfulness of the reception given his predecessor an atmosphere of festiveness permeated the city. Engravings by Weis depict Louis XV's arrival in the Rue du Vieux Marché-aux-Vins, the magnificent fireworks display before the Palais Rohan, jousting tournaments on the river Ill and the countless on-lookers massed at their windows and on rooftops.

They cannot of course render the smell of beef stuffed with rabbit and chicken that was grilled on the Place du Marché aux Herbes, today Place Gutenberg. Nor the gurgling libations that flowed from the wine fountains, shaped like swans, dolphins and women's busts, from which all drank joyfully. From the balcony of the recently-inaugurated Palais Rohan the king watched the sword dance given by the bakers' guild and the hoop dance of the coopers. In the morning he had attended a solemn mass in the cathedral, while in the evening he dined in the residence of Klinglin the Royal Intendant, which now houses the prefect's office.

Strasbourg had become the prestigious place of residence of the bishop prince and an important garrison town. After it surrendered to Louis XIV, Vauban had a citadel build – a real city within a city. Four to five thousand men were stationed in the numerous barracks, while outside on the street there was a highly diverse mix of French and German customs and dress. Women wearing the latest fashion and hair-dos from Paris mingled with those who still wore braids and dresses in the German style. The vivid colours of officers in military uniform contrasted starkly with the dark suits worn by members of the Magistrate in line with a long tradition of Protestant austerity.

Anonymous miniature paintings from 1614 depicting the peasants, nobles and merchants who made up the inhabitants of Strasbourg.

The new theatre built on the Place Broglie staged plays in French, while the Théâtre des Drapiers (Drapers Theatre) in the Grand Rue was devoted to German drama.

The churches of Saint-Pierre-le-Vieux et Saint-Pierre-le-Jeune had handed over their chancels to the Catholic faith and their naves to the Protestants. And the mausoleum of the Marshal of Saxony in 1777 was inaugurated by a ceremony at which Catholics and Protestants sat side by side in the church of Saint-

Thomas. The Protestant University was renowned for law and medicine. Professors continued to teach in latin and german, so drawing foreign students.

Cagliostro and the stirrings of revolution

In 1770 festivities once again enlivened Strasbourg's streets in honour of a visit from Marie-Antoinette. Among the crowds looking on was an unknown young student who followed events attentively. His

Page left: *Engraving by Weis showing the festivities which the city of Strasbourg held in honour of Louis XV's visit.*
Below: *Strasbourg's soldiers at the same period.*

name was Johann Wolfgang Goethe. He had come to study law in Strasbourg and had taken to frequenting the fashionable circles of the city. He would take his sweetheart with him. Her name was Frédérique Brion, but this daughter of protestant pastor Sassenheim – whose traditional German-style dress had delighted the young Goethe in the setting of a rural kirk – felt ill-at-ease in drawing rooms where high French fashion was the order of the day. And when she finally left him, Goethe felt as if a stone had been lifted from his heart, as he candidly admitted in his memoirs.

The city's dazzling high society drew many an adventurer. One was Casanova who stopped at the Hôtel de la Cour du Corbeau (Crow's Yard Hotel) in 1761 before heading for Augsburg in attractive company. Another, more significant, arrival was that of Cagliostro who entered the city in a black carriage drawn by six horses on 19th September, 1780. He excited much curiosity, preceded as he was by his reputation as a miraculous healer. He threw open his lodgings at number 7 Rue de la Râpe to rich and poor like. They flocked to him. A series of spectacular cures soon earned him growing popularity and the wrath of the local doctors.

The physicians' animosity did not affect him, however, for he was the favourite of the prince bishop, Cardinal Louis-René de Rohan. Madame de Genlis, governess of the children of the Duke of Orleans described the cardinal in these terms: "Prince Louis was pleasing to behold, too mannered for his position,

a frivolous, lively, witty conversationalist; he was not at all what he ought to have been, but he was as pleasing as one could be outside his rank and character."

Five years later when, as the royal chaplain, he was about to celebrate Assumption Mass at Versailles, he was arrested after becoming embroiled in the diamond necklace affair. An adventuress, Madame de la Motte, got him to acquire a diamond necklace for Queen Marie-Antoinette and faked a meeting with her. When the jeweler demanded payment the scandal broke. The queen's name was sullied and Cardinal de Rohan was arrested. Among the defendants in court was Cagliostro, whose chilling prediction that the King of France would be executed was soon to come true.

The birth of the Marseillaise

A painting by Isidore Pils in Strasbourg's History Museum depicts this scene: the French army officer and composer, Rouget de Lisle, has placed his hand on his heart and is lustily singing. The song was in fact the "*Marseillaise*", which was to become the French national anthem. Rouget de Lisle had written it on the night of the 25th to 26th April, 1792, in the drawing room of Mayor de Dietrich in City Hall on the Place Broglie. This account was contested by Dietrich's wife who wrote to her brother that her husband, the first mayor of Strasbourg, was also the first to sing the anthem in his fine tenor voice. He had commissioned it from the young Rouget de Lisle to commemorate the declaration of war against Austria a few days earlier.

What has come down to posterity was the intense emotion of that evening. Nineteenth-century Romantic poet, Lamartine, has described it in his "*Histoire des Girondins*" (History of the Girondines). "At the first verse faces paled, at the second tears flowed, at the last rapturous enthusiasm erupted. Dietrich, his wife, and the young officer fell weeping into each others' arms. The anthem of the fatherland had been found."

Printed copies of this martial chant were handed out to revolutionary forces marching from Marseilles to Paris. They entered the capital singing it and to this day is known as the "*Marseillaise*". Shortly afterwards Mayor Dietrich fell victim to the reign of Terror and was dismissed from office. The following year he was guillotined. Appointed Strasbourg's first mayor in 1790, he had played an important role when the Revolution broke out. On 21st July, 1789, when news of the taking of the Bastille was just reaching Strasbourg, he managed to avert disaster when crowds attacked and pillaged City Hall. He also organized a great patriotic banquet on 13th June, 1790 to fête the birth of the Revolutionary Federation of Rhineland. During the festivities two new-born babies were given the revolutionary names of "Federate" and "Civic". They were the first civil baptisms ever carried out in France. The ceremony took place on the Plaine des Bouchers and not in the cathedral which had been converted into a "temple of reason".

In 1793 the cathedral's spire was crowned with a gigantic Phrygian bonnet – the red caps of liberty worn by revolutionaries. Initially, a meeting of the Revolutionary Assembly had wanted to raze the steeple to the ground because it was an insult to the principle of equality. But the ironsmith Sulzer suggested capping it with red metal sheeting so that the triumph of the Revolution could be seen from afar. It remained in place until the very beginning of the 19th century.

In honor of Gutenberg

In 1801 a concordat determining the legal status of churches in Alsace-Lorraine, and still in force today, was signed by Pope Pius VII and Napoleon Bonaparte. Under Bonaparte Strasbourg flourished in many ways. The Rhône-to-Rhine Canal was built, as was the road bridge between Strasbourg and Kehl. After his triumph at Austerlitz, the Emperor visited Strasbourg to a delirious welcome. The city's old gates and the Place des Bouchers were all renamed Austerlitz. A grand ball given at the Hôtel de la Préfecture was immortalised in an engraving by Benjamin Zix, a painter and engraver from Strasbourg who followed the Emperor to most battlefields.

Empress Josephine visited Strasbourg for a second time in 1809, convening a grand ball to inaugurate an entertainment pavilion in the Parc de l'Orangerie. The Napoleonic era profoundly marked Strasbourg and all Alsace, whose patriotic zeal led it to supply France with one hundred and thirty-five generals. They included two famous Strasbourgeois – generals Kléber and Kellermann.

During the Napeleonic years the emperor's legend spread. Public fervour was such that images of him took many forms. Glass-mounted portraits were very popular and even the cast-iron plaques used to make the great stoves of Alsace were in the likeness of the emperor.

It was doubtless memories of this Napoleonic devotion that prompted Bonaparte's son, Prince Louis-Napoléon, to choose the Austerlitz Barracks in Strasbourg to foment his failed attempt at a *coup d'état* in 1836. It was the talking point for years in the *cafés*, *brasseries* and watering holes of the city.

One year of much festivity was 1840. On 14th June, forty years to the day after his assassination in Cairo, the statue of General Kléber was at last revealed to the public. Only ten days later a ceremony held from 23rd to 25th June marked the unveiling of the statue of

CHEMINS DE FER DE PARIS A STRASBOURG.

"More an apparition than a portrait" was how David d'Angers' statue of Gutenberg on the square of the same name was described for the strength and wisdom of the inventor of printing that it expresses.

Gutenberg. "For three days a tide of gladness rippled through the entire city of Strasbourg," wrote the sculptor David d'Angers, who created the work free of charge. He went on: "The authorities merely looked on, it was truly the people who benefited from the festivities." The Parisian press of the time, such as *Le Courrier français* and *Le Siècle*, were lavish in their praise of a ceremony that was both rooted in the people and international in scope. A *cortège industriel*, made up of craftsmen in full costume marched through the city's streets. Printers, book-sellers and smelters from Paris, Lyon and as far afield as Rio de Janeiro took part in this great event, at which everybody who was anybody in the French literary world was present. Victor Hugo, president of the Société des Lettres (Literary Society), sent a delegation to Strasbourg where it met up with members of the Académie Française. The statue – also widely marketed as a miniature – caused a stir. It was described as "more an apparition than a portrait", while another comment from the time was: "Gutenberg has the fantastical look of those doctors from the Middle Ages who stand half-way between magic and science." Public figures and journalists from Paris had to make the journey in stage coach. There was no railway line from the capital to Strasbourg until July 1852, when it was finally inaugurated by Prince Louis-Napoléon, who had at last become president following a successful coup attempt on 2nd December, 1851. In 1870, he declared himself Napoleon III at the head of a "parliamentary Empire". A few months later the Franco-Prussian War broke out, leading to his downfall.

A rain of fire, iron and steel

In the night of 25th August the cry, "the cathedral is burning" went up from the streets and it was true. Projectiles crammed with incendiary substances had pierced the copper plates that formed the roof of the nave and set fire to the forest of beams which supported it. It was a spectacle that was both terrifying and horrible, and yet it was somehow magnificent to behold from afar the savage grandeur of those masses of molten metal twisting in the flames and dripping from on high in bluish trails, while the stonework balustrades, cornices and statuettes fell with a rending sound and shattered on the ground," related one eye-witness, the historian Rodolphe Reuss in his "History of Strasbourg".

The siege of Strasbourg by Bismarck's army began on 8th August, 1870. Before that had come the defeats at Woerth and Froeschwiller. The people of the city had watched as France's armoured cavalry had plodded on foot and bare-headed back into the city through the gates of Pierre and Saverne. They were followed by bedraggled gunners and infantrymen.

Nobody believed the enemy would bombard the city. But nobody knew the determination of Prussian General von Werder. He had decided to bring the city to its knees as fast as possible at any price. He stationed his artillery batteries at Kehl, Hausbergen, Schiltigheim and Elsau and in August they began firing – sporadically, at first, then intensively, like on the nights of the 24th and 26th. The whistling of shells became a daily sound. They landed all over the city, causing fires to break out. In addition to the cathedral, the Aubette, City Hall, theatre, Œuvre Notre-Dame and the prefecture were all hit.

There were irreparable losses including that of the library in the former Dominican convent. Thousands of

Page left: *Drawing of the snowbound Place Kléber from a children's book.*
Above: *The bombardment of Strasbourg in 1870.*

GLOIRE AUX VAINQUEURS

manuscripts, early printed books and other priceless works went up in smoke. They included the famous *Hortus Deliciarum* by the mother superior of the Convent of Mount Saint Odile, Herrade de Landsberg. It was a veritable encyclopaedia of 12th century lore and boasted a wealth of illuminations. The number of civilian casualties grew daily. The dead were buried in the botanical garden which is today part of the School of Decorative Arts. Opposite the ornamental pond covered with water lilies redolent of a Japanese etching stands a rock monument to the dead of 1870 who are buried there. Altogether there were 280 deaths, 1,500 wounded and 10,000 homeless. When the city's fortified walls were breached on 27th September, General Uhrich, commander of the French forces, knew that any further resistance was hopeless. The following day he signed the act of surrender in the railway station at Koenigshoffen. A painting by Théophile Schuler shows Mayor Kuss standing before the city's smoking ruins. The mayor, a medical professor, had spared no effort in trying to help the stricken inhabitants, who were soon to be cut down by a typhoid epidemic. Together with other local officials, he went to Bordeaux, where the National Assembly had reconvened, to protest against the annexation of Alsace-Lorraine. In vain, though, as a majority of parliamentarians agreed to it. Under the terms of the Treaty of Frankfurt, on 10th May, 1871, Alsace, Lorraine and the Moselle were all signed over to Germany, which made them part of the Reichsland. A moving short story by Alphonse Daudet, entitled the "The last class", tells the tale of a school teacher who bids farewell to his pupils in their last lesson in French before a German teacher takes over. In later years a sense of Alsatian identity would develop in young generations, giving rise to an intellectual revival that was to spawn the museum and theatre of Alsace as well as regionally specific creative writing.

"Humans 40, horses lengthwise 8"

Cats, nothing but cats in the otherwise deserted streets of the city: black-and-white photographs of the winter of 1939-1940 tell their own story. Strasbourg had been evacuated in early September. The streets were

empty of people, cars and sledges, while the glass roof of the cathedral had been planked over. The statue of Kléber, like other monuments had been sandbagged. On the other side of France in the southwestern town of Périgueux a great Christmas tree shimmered on the main street, the Cours Montaigne. It was there that over 11,000 Strasbourgeois had taken refuge after the evacuation order on 2nd September. Some were still reeling from the shock of seeing the posters issued by the War Ministry telling the city's inhabitants to go to various assembly points the following day. They were allowed 30 kilos of belongings, no more, enough food for four days and would be issued with refugee cards. They would be taken to their destination by specially requisitioned goods trains dating back to 1914. On some wagons there still hung plaques with the instruction, Humans 40, horses lengthwise 8.

The Strasbourgeois who quit their city in September 1939 experienced a true exodus and the fate of refugees, whoever they are, can no longer leave them indifferent. Not all were evacuated to the Dordogne; some were sent to the Haute-Vienne in

central France, while Strasbourg University moved to Clermont-Ferrand in the Massif Central. The young Alsatians were doubtless thrilled to discover new regions and soon got over being called *Ja-jas*. Their elders, however, felt the pull of home and the communication barrier between the new arrivals and local inhabitants sprang not only from linguistic differences. Strong bonds of friendship were, of course, formed, but the refugees were assailed by mixed feelings. Nobody has expressed them better than playwright Germain Muller in his play *Enfin redde m'r nim devon* (Let's not talk about it). He wrote it when he was twenty-one and it includes this dialogue between an Alsatian father and his Perigordian landlady

"Mme Chapoulard (the Meyers' landlady): Well… now well I was thinking… I was thinking that now the war's over–

Meyer: We're not going back to Alsace!

Mme Chapoulard: Oh and why not?

Meyer: Because of the Germans.

Mme Chapoulard: Monsieur Meyer, what are you complaining about. You people are always on the winning side.

Meyer: That depends on your point of view.

Mme Chapoulard: After all, everyone goes on about the Germans, but they are people just like us. Even Marshall Pétain said we've got to learn to get on with them, we've got to collaborate. He said the war was over, didn't he? Look, Monsieur Meyer, you wouldn't be happy here.

Meyer: We live in times, Madame Chapoulard, when we shouldn't seek to be happy but not to be too unhappy.

Mme Chapoulard: That's nonsense, all that! This is my home here. And anyway the Germans aren't like real foreigners for you. They understand you, and you lot with your mentality understand them better than we do. You can speak French, but the other ja-jas who chew on straw all day long, don't you think they'd be better off back where they come from, even with the Germans?"

Below: *In September, 1940, street and shop names were changed as they had been in 1918. They were not to become French again until 1944.*
Page right: *On 26th November 1944 the Place Kléber was the scene of General Leclerc's victory ceremony in newly liberated Strasbourg.*

In the wake of the Armistice of 22nd June, 1940, three-quarters of the people of Strasbourg returned to the city. It was a grim shock for the first arrivals on 6th August to see their city emblazoned with swastikas, as it would be for another four years. Two years later, on 25th August, 1942, forcible conscription began for the young men of Alsace. Among the 130,000 who left to fight, 32,000 are estimated to have lost their lives and 10,500 disappeared.

The red poster

At six o'clock on the morning of 15th July, 1943, six young Alsatian men were shot by a firing squad in Desaix Fort. Red posters stuck on the walls of the city at dawn read: "Condemned to death and stripped of all civic rights on 7th July, 1943, by the people's court for incitement to treason, complicity with the enemy and crimes against the state's external security: Alphonse Adam, 24, of Strasbourg-Schiltigheim, Robert Kieffer, 23, of Bischheim, Pierre Tschaen, 21, of Strasbourg, Charles Schneider, 25, of Altwiller,

Joseph Seger, 47, of Petit Landau, Robert Meyer, 28, of Strasbourg, were executed today. Berlin, 15th July, 1943. Signed: the Public prosecutor of the Reich at the People's Court."

The trial began on 6th July before a packed Strasbourg courtroom. More than one hundred of the defendant's sympathizers were there. Although they knew full well that they were surrounded by plainclothes Gestapo agents, they openly demonstrated support for their thirty comrades, who all belonged to the Front de la Jeunesse Alsacienne (Alsatian Youth Front), founded in the autumn of 1941 by Alphonse Adam and Robert Kieffer. The main charge was that they had helped escaped prisoners of war and young Alsatians fleeing draft over the Vosges Mountains into Free France. But they also stood accused of distributing pamphlets urging the local youth not to report to the conscription bureau and of printing special ID cards for the forced draftees on which it was specified in three languages that the card bearer was French and should be treated as an ally.

The trumped-up trial lasted for two days and the main prosecuting lawyer was Roland Freisler, who the next year in Berlin was to secure the death sentence for the 100 accomplices of 20th of July, following the assassination attempt on Hitler. The heat and tension were extreme. On the second day of the trial a tremendous storm broke out which plunged the courtroom into darkness. Six of the accused were sentenced to death and on the morrow of their execution, the local Nazi newspaper ran the headline: "Traitors eradicated in Alsace".

Other resistants also suffered. One was the group headed by Marcel Weinum, who was axed to death at the age of 17 in Stuttgart in 1942. Not to mention Lucie Welschinger, the Bareiss Network and Commander François, whose real name was Georges Kiefer. He was to become leader of the Resistance of the Lower Rhine.

There is a whole district in the Neuhof neigh-bourhood whose street names perpetuate the memory of the time and the resistance members. Some of them are well known, others less so. Who remembers Raoul Clainchard, killed at 25, in a prison in Stuttgart? Yet he was one of those who paid with his life.

Strasbourg liberated

General Leclerc had hoped to liberate Strasbourg on 22nd November like General Gouraud had in 1918. He was one day out, but he kept the pledge he had obtained from his troops on capturing Kufra during the North African campaign: "Swear to lay down your

arms only when our great colors will float over Strasbourg Cathedral."

On 23rd November, 1944, at 9.30 a.m. the first units of the Second Armored Division entered the city by the Place de Haguenau. The code message "*Tissu est dans iode*" (cloth is in iodine), signifying the success of the operation, was sent out. Other battalions entered the city by the Rhineland docks. By 2 p.m. the *tricolore* was floating over the cathedral. Yet victory was far from secured. For three days snipers and German batteries on the other side of the Rhine kept up the pressure on the city. Faced with broadside against the Palais du Rhin where he first set up his headquarters, General Leclerc decided to move them to Esca (premises of the

Est–capital company). That is where he received notification of the surrender of the commander of the local German forces, General Vaterrodt. And on 26th November, despite the danger from eight Messerschmidts wheeling overhead a military parade on the Place Kléber formalised victory.

Strasbourg was not yet liberated, however. A strong German offensive had prompted fierce fighting in the Ardennes and the allies asked Leclerc's second armoured division to quit Strasbourg to provide reinforcements. He left on 30th December. From then until 4th January the city was defended only by two squadrons of riot police, the resistance forces of the FFI and the Brigade d'Alsace-Lorraine.

The brigade had been created by Colonel Berger, better known as André Malraux. In support of General Lattre he disposed his one thousand men along the Rhine. They defended the stretch from Gambsheim to Rhinau and paid a heavy price in the process. General De Gaulle had to intervene to prevent the allies from abandoning Strasbourg, as he relates in his "Mémoires de Guerre": "The evacuation of Alsace, and especially of its capital city, might have seemed logical from the point of view of the Allies' strategy. But France could not accept […] That Strasbourg should be defended was what I first had to secure. To be sure that this would indeed be done, I had no choice but to issue orders to that effect to the 1st French Army. On 1st January, I transmitted my instructions to General de Lattre."

Strasbourg was liberated for the second and last time on 18th January, 1945, thanks to the mettle of French combatants who fought with grim determination.

Below: Général Leclerc's proclamation sinks in.

5

Literary Ghosts

"There may be no surer way of understanding a city's personality than to explore the special relation that such and such an artist has enjoyed with it."

Roland Recht

Above: La Construction de la cathédrale *painted by Théophile Schuler in the 19th century.*
Page right, above: *A room in the Hotel Oesinger recreates the atmosphere of a writer's studio in the Palais Rohan. Below: The facades of the Aubette music hall that give on to the Rue du Vieux Marché-aux-Poissons and Place Kléber have medallions commemorating visits from Goethe and Mozart.*

There are cities whose sheer beauty has inspired young writers to poignant despair. Prague is one, eliciting sadness in a story by the great early 20th century French poet Guillaume Apollinaire and a sense of solitude in Albert Camus's unpublished first novel "A Happy Death". Strasbourg, however, has inspired a lust for life in artists.

Goethe, who arrived in April, 1770, to study law, was instantly fired with enthusiasm. He wrote: "I had taken a room at the Inn of the Spirit; and, to slake my most ardent wish, I dashed forthwith to the cathedral." Admittedly, he recounted this memory when he was in his 60s and looking back on his youth in the "Dichtung und Wahrheit" volume of his memoirs. He was laden with honors and duties at the Weimar court and the long-gone Strasbourg years must have seemed like a paradise lost.

When he was actually in Strasbourg as a young man he wrote a more wary letter to his friend Limprecht: "The city has some aspects which can set the soul in motion, release it from its habitual state, and drive it both to heights and to depths." But for the young student who was inquisitive about everything, there was so much to explore in Strasbourg. Initially he was not driven by his passion for law, the subject he was

studying, even if he was to admit: "Jurisprudence begins to please me a great deal. So it is with all things, such as the beer in Strasbourg; it revolts us the first time that we drink it, but after we have been drinking it for more than one week, we can no longer do without."

Goethe and Mozart at Large

Under the influence of fellow lodgers at the Lauth sisters' boarding house in the Rue de l'Ail (Garlic Street), he developed a passion for medicine. He attended Professor Ehrmann's dissections in the small

Below: Hôtel de l'Esprit, *a 19th century engraving by B. Zix.*
Facing: *The* "Maison aux Trois Lièvres" *(Three Hare House) at 19* Rue de l'Ail *(Garlic Street), where Goethe's friend, Jung-Stilling, a German mystic lived.*
Below: *Pietsch's 19th century lithography,* Goethe in Strasbourg.

chapel of Saint Erhardt's hospital, where a sign put up in 1740 bears the inscription *Theatrum Anatomicum.*

Also something of a socialite, Goethe attended dance classes to learn steps that would be useful in the salons of high society. The cathedral, too, was an endless source of both aesthetic and physical enrichment. To vanquish his fear of heights he regularly forced himself to climb to the very top of the spire, putting into practice (as he always would) a

precept he had spelled out in a letter to Schiller: "I hate all that merely instructs me, that which fails to enrich my capacity for action does not instill in me an instant rush of life." Never again, except maybe during his travels in Italy, did Goethe experience such a keen sense of freedom.

Seven years later another young genius was to experience a similar sentiment in Strasbourg. He was Mozart. After an inconclusive sojourn in Paris he was heading back to Salzburg where he was once again to be the bishop's "musical valet". His impresario in Paris, Baron Grimm, had told Mozart's father that he would provide for him as far as Strasbourg. His father then had to find the fare from Strasbourg to Salzburg.

The 22-year-old Mozart's first impressions were not exactly uplifting as he arrived in a poor carriage, the cheapest that his penny-pinching impresario could find. After Paris and Nancy, the Palais Rohan and town mansions left him cold. But in the ensuing month he was to change his mind. Although they did not exactly flock to his concerts, Strasbourg's music-lovers played a part in his change of heart. "Their sheer applause and cheering deafened my ears as much as if the hall had been full," he wrote on 26th October, 1778. A few days later he added, in a similar vein: "On 31st October, my name day, I enjoyed myself for two hours or, to be precise, I brought enjoyment to others."

At one point he considered not returning to Salzburg, but staying on in Strasbourg to become master of the cathedral's chapel in place of Jean-Xavier Richter. Ignace Pleyel ultimately secured the position and Mozart went on his way, although not before writing to his father that Strasbourg could no longer do without him: "You cannot believe how well I am considered here or how much I am loved."

*Mozart socialised intensively in Strasbourg. He had access not just
to the organ in Temple Neuf but to the musical evenings of high society.*
Left: *Melling's* Portrait of Two spouses: the de Dietrich Family, *1776.*
Below: La Belle Strasbourgeoise *by N. de Largillière, 1703.*
Below: *J.-A. Silberman's 18th century drawing of the case
of the organ Temple Neuf.*

The Romantic Border

In the first half of the 19ᵗʰ century all the great French and German Romantic writers spent time in Strasbourg. Never had a city touched chords so close to the contemporary imagination. It had everything – the Gothic style of its cathedral, the legend-laden atmosphere of its old quarters and the mythical attraction of the Rhine, a compulsory staging post on any writer's European journey. Grand, well tended streets lined with private palaces, like the Rue du Dôme, which the poet and novelist Gérard de Nerval

compared to Paris's stately Rue Vivienne (then home to the Bibliothèque Nationale), stood cheek-by-jowl with mazes of winding lanes. Seven medieval gates still guarded the entrance to a city interlaced by a network of canals. The largest of them was the Fossé des Tanneurs (Tanners' Ditch), as evil-smelling as it was picturesque. It had not yet been covered over, so possibly contributed to Gerard de Nerval's sense that Strasbourg had a – literally ! – overpowering air of the Middle Ages.

De Nerval, whom the acerbic literary critic Sainte-Beuve dubbed the "Paris to Munich travelling

salesman", discovered Strasbourg in 1838. He was joined by Alexandre Dumas with whom he was working jointly on a play entitled "Léo Burckhardt". In that same year he shed his real name, Gérard Labrunie, and assumed his *nom de plume*, Gérard de Nerval.

He was to describe his first – and by no means his last – visit to Strasbourg in vivid detail in a piece called "Lorely". As soon as had checked in to the Hôtel de la Cour du Corbeau (Crow's Yard Hotel) his first impulse was to see the Rhine. Although, at the tender age of 20 he had translated "Faust" so brilliantly that he had won Goethe's admiration, he rushed out to visit not the Cathedral, but the river, this border between the two Romanticisms. He was, however, a little disappointed. "You understand that the first thought of a Parisian alighting from his coach at Strasbourg is to ask his way to the Rhine. Soon he is astounded to learn that the Rhine is a further league outside the city. What, the Rhine does not lap at the walls of Strasbourg or at those of its old cathedral? Alas, no. The Rhine in Strasbourg and the sea in Bordeaux are the two great mistakes of the sedentary Parisian. But, regardless of fatigue from the journey, how can one spend even an hour in Strasbourg without having seen the Rhine? So one crosses half of the city, wends one's way across the fortifications, then follows the roadway for half a league, and finally the city behind disappears entirely save for the stone finger of the steeple. When one has crossed the first arm of the Rhine, which is as wide as the Seine, and an island green with poplars and birches, one then sees the great river tumbling swiftly by and bearing in its grey tears an eternal storm." And, he adds, in a burst of enthusiasm. "But over there on the horizon, over the moving pontoon of sixty ships, do you know what that is? Germany! The land of Goethe and Schiller, the land of Hoffmann: old Germany, mother of us all!... Teutonia."

He was not alone in his passion for the Rhine. Victor Hugo followed in de Nerval's footsteps in September the following year. In his book, "The Rhine: A Tour from Paris to Mainz by Way of Aix-la-Chapelle", he asserts: "Of all rivers it is the Rhine I love." Strasbourg is the subject of two chapters of the work, made up of letters that recount each stage in his journey.

Romantic Travelogue

Unlike de Nerval, Victor Hugo was no stroller. The author of "*Notre-Dame de Paris*", shortly to be received into the illustrious fold of the Académie Française, was a traveler in a hurry. He liked to go the heart of a place, omitting nothing on the way.

He begins with a description of Place Kléber, then Place d'Armes. Maison Rouge, the hotel where he stayed, looked on to the square. "Here I am in Strasbourg, my friend," he wrote. "To my right I have a clump of trees, to my left the Munster, whose bells are at full peal at the moment, in front a 16th century house that is very beautiful, albeit daubed with yellow paint and green shutters; behind are the high gables of an old nave, wherein is the city's library; in the middle of the square a wooden hut from which will rise, I am told, a monument to Kléber."

Like the many Romantics who were to come after him – from Lamartine and Vigny to George Sand and Musset – he made a point of climbing the steps up to the flat roof of the cathedral, which he described as "a prodigy of the gigantic and the delicate". He signed the visitors' book.

Another compulsory exercise of the time was to pass comment on the funeral monument to Marshal de Saxe, sculpted by Pigalle. Gérard de Nerval adopted a gently mocking tone, saying the statue produced the effect of "the commander from Don Juan: one is tempted to invite him to supper". Only Stendhal appreciated it: "It derives its effect from the sculptor's daring to be dramatic. There is movement which gives his face expression. The marshal steps into an open grave with a superbly intrepid face."

Victor Hugo praised what he liked – the cathedral – with the same passion that he denigrated what he

Page left: *The* Auberge de la Fleur *(Flower Inn)*
in Rue de la Douane *was very animated in the 19th century.*
Below: *Stepping on to the jetty towards the Rue de Rohan.*

disliked, namely the tomb. He described it as "that much famed, much vaunted and deeply mediocre thing. It is a great marble machine in the meagre style of Pigalle."

Balzac's Sacred Cities

A few years later it was the turn of Balzac and his "beautiful stranger", the Polish countess, Eva Hanska, to sojourn in the Alsatian capital. It was Eva's first encounter with France. The two lovers feared trouble crossing the border, for Czarist Russia did not take kindly travellers to France – a revolutionary, turbulent land. Balzac therefore took care to acquire forged passports in which he passed Eva Hanska and her

daughter Anna off as his sister and niece. He had already made a reconnaissance trip on 22nd June, 1845. But he had nothing to fear. "Nobody asks to see passports anywhere," he wrote reassuringly to his beloved.

On 7th July, after a trouble-free trip they arrived by mail coach in Strasbourg and checked in at the Auberge de la Fleur (Flower Inn) at 13 Rue de la Douane. For the couple it was the beginning of a long trek across Europe that would take them in Baden-Baden, Naples, Rome, Rotterdam, Brussels, Vienna, Antwerp, Toulon and Paris. In all, the lovers visited twenty-three cities that Balzac considered sacred. He rated each in terms of his emotional journey with Eva Hanska. Of Strasbourg he wrote:

"Our love is already learned, as rich as Louis XV, mutual happiness is a certainty."

Balzac used his stay in Strasbourg to show Eva round the city with which he was already familiar. He led her off the beaten track to the church of Saint-Pierre-le-Jeune and into the gloom of the little Trinity Chapel, lit only by the soft light through its stained-glass-windows. It was there that the two lovers promised each other that they would become engaged, as Balzac recalled in a letter of 12th August, 1846: "From the day when, as we have done since Strasbourg, we took each other's hands in that little chapel...I will remain faithful as you intend."

When the Strasbourg-Paris railway line opened in 1852, Strasbourg lost a little of its mystique as a voyage of initiation. It now took only a dozen hours to get there. The staging posts of the mail coach were a thing of the past, as were the bumpy roads and the overnight stops in the inns that Stendhal described on his frequent visits to Strasbourg as supplies officer with the Napeoleonic army. The chummy chats with customs officers that Théophile Gauthier recounted were a thing of the past. Now that it was easy, the trip to Strasbourg had become mundane. The city would reassert its attraction as a frontier post only after the Prussian siege of 1870. Following the city's annexation its first illustrious visitors included Richard Wagner, his wife Cosima and Frederick Nietzsche who spent the night of 23rd November, 1872, at the *Hôtel de la Ville de Paris*.

Tramways and Biplanes

Some half-century later, in 1923, a 24-year-old journalist devoted a long piece to Strasbourg among his other articles, which included the Genoa Conference, American bohemia in Paris, an earthquake in Japan and a penetrating portrait of Mussolini. The reporter's name was Ernest Hemingway, then correspondent for the *Toronto Daily Star*. He flew to Strasbourg from Paris in a two-seater propeller-driven aeroplane on his way to Germany to report on the effects of galloping inflation. He painted a minutely detailed picture of the city which he crossed by tram to get to Kehl. The sheer wealth of his description makes the reader feel a passenger on the tram clanging its way through the early morning.

CH. WINTER phot.

71

"On the front platform of the streetcar, with a little ticket window opening into the car through which the conductor accepted a franc for myself and the two bags, we clanged along through the winding streets of Strasbourg and the early morning. There were sharp-peaked plastered houses criss-crossed with great wooden beams; the river wound and rewound through the town and each time we crossed it there were fishermen on the banks, there was the wide modern street with modern German shops with big glass show windows and new French names over their doors, butchers were unshuttering their shops and with their assistants hanging the big carcasses of beeves and horses outside the doors, a long stream of carts were coming into market from the country, streets were being flushed and washed. I caught a glimpse down a side street of the great red stone cathedral. There was a sign in French and another in German forbidding anyone to talk to the motorman and the motorman chatted in French and German to his friends who got on the car

as he swung his levers and checked or speeded our progress along the narrow streets and out of the town."

A year earlier, the discovery of Strasbourg had been a far more decisive experience for a group of young people of the same age. It was at the city's Polygone Aerodrome that Antoine de Saint-Exupéry passed his pilot's licence at the controls of a single-seater Spad. He wrote to his mother: "Strasbourg is an exquisite town. All the characteristics of a big city."

It was here that André Malraux, at the behest of his new wife, Clara, spent his honeymoon. Little did he know, as he strolled around the cathedral, that he would one day hear the most moving Te Deum of his life there. It would be on 17th December, 1944 in thanksgiving for the end of four years of war and oppression. Bombing raids would have devastated the crossing tower, blown out the stained glass windows and opened the nave to the elements.

A Climb-And-A-Half

The most jubilatory piece of writing inspired by the cathedral was doubtless by Elias Canetti in 1933. He already enjoyed a considerable reputation as an intellectual in Vienna, even though his novel "Auto-Da-Fé", still a manuscript in his desk, was not to be published until three years later and his Nobel Prize for Literature would come only in 1981. He was in Strasbourg attending a contemporary music festival at the invitation of the great conductor Hermann Scherchen and had booked into the old *Hôtel du Louvre* in the room where Herder had once welcomed Goethe.

Scherchen gave Canetti a copy of the "L'almanach des muses", a book of rare poetry which included one of Lenz's earlier pieces. No gift could have given Canetti such pleasure, for he was passionately fond of German Preromantism. He was also, like Goethe, fascinated by the cathedral. "But my great experience

during those weeks so full of people, smells and sounds was climbing to the top of the Cathedral," he wrote in "The Play of the Eyes", the third volume of his autobiography. "This I did every day, omitting none. I did not climb slowly and patiently, I was in a hurry to reach the platform and was out of breath when I got there. A day that didn't begin with this climb was for me no day at all, and I counted the days according to my visits to the Cathedral tower. Accordingly I spent more days in Strasbourg than there were in the month, for sometimes I succeeded, in the spite of all there was to hear, in visiting the tower in the afternoon as well. I envied the man who lived up there, for he had a head start on the long way up the winding stairs. I had fallen in love with the view of the mysterious city rooftops and with every stone that I grazed in climbing."

The young Canetti, then aged 28, went on to add prophetically: "I saw the Vosges and the Black Forest together, and made no mistake about what divided them in this year. The war that had ended fifteen years before still weighed on my mind, and I felt that before many years there would be another."

Great Affection for Strasbourg

As war correspondent for the newspaper, *Intransigeant*, Pierre Demarchay, better known as the novelist Pierre Mac Orlan, had witnessed with his own eyes the French army's entry into Strasbourg in November 1918. When he returned in 1934, it was to carry out a reportage for the magazine *Détective* on an unusual topic entitled "The Strasbourg Experiment". The experiment was the closure of the city's brothels. It was the first measure of this type taken in France since 1925 and it preceded by 20 years the Marthe Richard Act which closed brothels much implicated in collaboration with the Nazi occupier. The Prefect, had taken the decision following a scandal that had rocked Strasbourg. The 47th Federal and National Gymnastics

festival in the city had attracted some twelve thousand athletes, most of whom were very young. Yet performances were conspicuously low and brothel custom particularly high.

Ten years later Mac Orlan drew mixed conclusions about the effectiveness of closing down the brothels. Prostitution had gone underground and assumed a new form in the shape of "tea rooms" that were in essence little different. Mac Orlan (on whose novel "Quai des Brumes" Marcel Carné's eponymous film was based) was a great lover of cities with docks and ports. His reportage was chiefly an opportunity for him to sing the praises of Strasbourg, whose Gemütlichkeit, or "chumminess" he was keen to share.

"When I enter Strasbourg, I would like decent types to recognise me with a little start of surprise. Look, he's back! they would say. When I stay in Strasbourg, I try as I can to slip into the ordinary life of the community. I buy ties just for the pleasure of talking to the salesgirl. I like to find out whether she hails from the locality and I come back shortly afterwards to buy something else. I seek any pretext, when I take my leave, not to put too sudden a stop to the sheer gaiety that tinges young girls' faces pink. Then I walk off to the station, taking with me something heavier than my luggage. Quite frankly, I cannot explain this great affection I feel for Strasbourg. It seems to me that I have long lived in the city and that the picturesqueness which so delights tourists does not surprise me for that very reason. When I wander along the waterfront not far from the Maison du Corbeau, which contains an admirable collection of regimental souvenirs, I find myself lending an ear just to catch cosy, familiar phrases, like: 'It's old Mac. Only yesterday he was down at Beer Palace.' – 'I'm meeting him tonight at the Aubette [music hall]'."

Mac Orlan's reportages bathe in a dream-like atmosphere. Collected in his book, "Rues Secrètes" (Secret Streets), they are like a veritable prose poem in praise of Strasbourg.

6

Tradition of Invention

"Strasbourg, for which one leaves without regret all other cities and which is, for the thinking mind, a capital city."
Numa Denis Fustel de Coulanges

The time has come to provide the keys which unlock Strasbourg and the secret of its attraction, due in part to its heritage and cultural wealth but also to something more intangible: its creative energy. The city whose cathedral spire thrusts powerfully skyward has been the crucible for numerous inventions over the centuries. The one which has undoubtedly most affected the course of all history is the printing press with its movable metal characters. For over 10 years, it was in Strasbourg that the obscure Johan Gensfleich, known as Gutenberg, laboured painstakingly over his invention. It was also in Strasbourg that a passionate young scientist, named Louis Pasteur, conducted the experiments that were to lead to a rabies vaccine and save countless lives. Today in the three universities, schools and private companies of Greater Strasbourg five thousand researchers are at work. Many practical applications have resulted thanks to backing from major international corporations like Roche, Lilly, Synthélabo Biomoléculaire, Transgène, General Motors and Delphi. They chose to open facilities in Strasbourg precisely because it offers an environment that is conducive to the advance of research. Every year the Strasbourg branch of France's National Institute of Industrial Property (INPI) registers some 150 patents, of which a dozen originate from the University of Louis Pasteur, acknowledged as one of France's top research centres.

A project to build a new museum complex that will be known as the "Science Garden" is currently in the planning stage. The aim is to throw open to the general public the world and work of science, so often shrouded in anonymity. Names have nevertheless broken into this on 16 occasions – when Nobel Prizes have been awarded to Strasbourg-based scientists, such as Alfred Kastler and Jean-Marie Lehn.

Page left: *The mechanism of the Astronomical Clock, built between 1571 and 1574 in a formidable feat of engineering.*
Right: *Extract from the first Bible printed by Gutenberg in 1454.*

Below: *Inside the Astronomical Clock the 12 apostles dance in an eternal ring.*

Gutenberg, inventor of books for all

Visitors strolling along the banks of the Ill might notice a tiny islet scarcely large enough to hold the upright pink sandstone slab and bench that stand in the shade of a poplar tree. The islet is called the Montagne Verte, or Green Mountain. An inscription carved in the slab reads: "It is here on the Montagne Verte that printing was discovered by Jean Gutenberg. It is from here that, through printing, light shone on the world."

When Johan Gensfleich, alias Gutenberg, arrived in Strasbourg in 1344, or thereabouts, he came as a total stranger. All that was known about him was that unrest had compelled him to leave his native town of Mainz, where he belonged to a patrician family that had taken its name from its home, "zum Gutenberg". To pursue his research in the utmost secrecy he needed to find a hideaway. At the time, the church of Saint Arbogast stood on the island of Montagne Verte. Attached to it was an abandoned monastery and Gutenberg probably

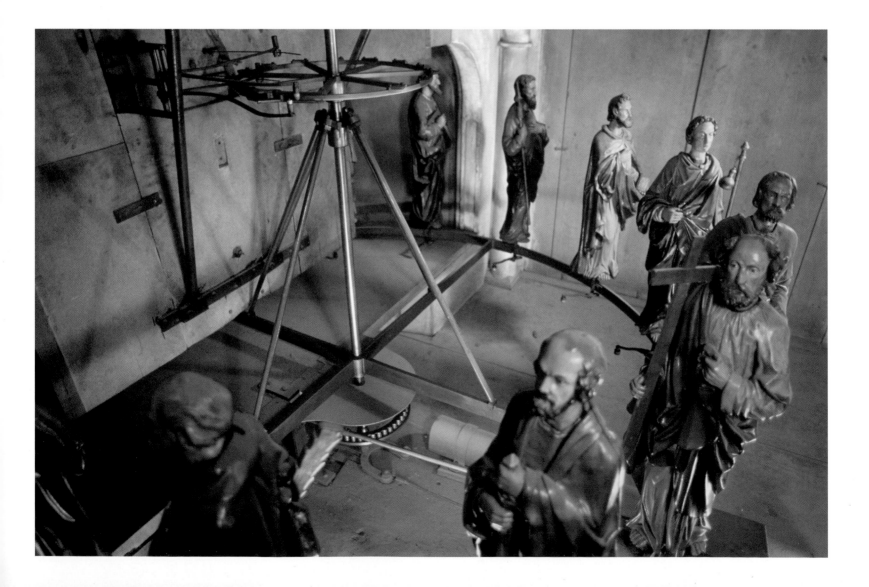

set up his first workshop in one of its disused outhouses. He earned his living by polishing precious stones and making salvation mirrors for pilgrims designed to catch blessed emanations from the holy relics at Aachen. Yet mystery continues to shroud his abiding passion – the creation of a mechanical writing system, to which he gave the code name, "Kunst und Adventur".

Whether he was a crazed adventurer or visionary of genius nobody yet knew. But his turbulent personality certainly had tongues wagging in Strasbourg. The documentary evidence that he resided in Strasbourg until 1444 comes not from the City Archives, burnt in 1870, but from copies made by the historian Jean-Daniel Schoepflin. From them we learn, among other things, that one Ennelin zu der Iseren Thür (Emily Iron Door) lodged a complaint against him with the church tribunal for an unkept marriage pledge, that an invoice testifies to an annual wine consumption of 1,924 litres and that he owed 80 florins to the chapter of Saint-Thomas. The minutes of a court case shed additional light on the invention on which he worked in his hideaway on the Montagne Verte. The case involved Gutenberg and the brother of one his partners, André Dritzehn, who met with sudden death on Christmas evening 1438. The court called no less than thirty three witnesses during the trial, where there was much oblique reference to formes, molten lead, matrices, screws and to a printing press that was hurriedly dismantled on the night in question.

The famous, perfectly executed 42-line Bible appeared in Mainz in 1454, but Strasbourg was the scene of all the necessary preparatory work – the design and production of the manual letterpress, the metal alloys, the choice of inks and paper types – which led to the invention of the printing press with its movable metal characters.

The invention aroused an enormous response in Strasbourg. A score of printers swiftly opened workshops.

In terms of quality and the scope of distribution, Jean Mentelin was among the first of the city's printers to gain renown abroad. Religious works, the classics of Antiquity and medical treatises illustrated by etchings were dispatched by boat to neighbouring countries. The momentum was never to cease. Over the next centuries many famous authors, from Voltaire to Rainer-Maria Rilke, would come to Strasbourg in search of a printer.

From Paracelsus to Remote Surgery

Among the works coveted by numerous scholars was a treatise on surgery by Hieronymus Brunschwig published in 1497. Paracelsus, one of the Renaissance's most famous and most controversial doctors, settled in Strasbourg in 1526 and sought to have his book on surgery printed. He well knew that Strasbourg had a surgeon's school which held that surgery was the equal of other branches of medicine – something almost unheard of at the time.

In 1728 another Strasbourg pioneer, Jean-Jacques Fried, created the first school for midwives and the first obstetrics teaching hospital in Europe.

In 1921 the regional daily, *Dernières Nouvelles d'Alsace,* conducted a survey on the theme "Which Alsatian has rendered the greatest service to humanity?" Eugène Koeberlé came in an easy first, well ahead of the pastor Oberlin and Pope Leon IX.

Koeberlé, who pioneered modern surgery, spent his entire working career in Strasbourg. In 1863 he carried out the first hysterectomy in France. Well before Pasteur, he believed firmly that hygiene played an important role in the success of operations and operated in an aseptic theatre. He invented numerous surgical instruments and when he could not design and make them himself, he entrusted the job to a cutler in the Rue Mercière. His "hemostatic forceps with ratchet lock", which was intended "to undertake without loss of blood the most serious operations and achieve the closure of the widest wounds", has become a universal classic in its different forms.

But who, then, could have guessed that one day new technology would enable a surgical team in New York to operate on a patient in Strasbourg? This premiere in surgical history was the work of Professor Marescaux and his team from the Institute of Research into Cancers of the Digestive Tract (IRCAD) in 2001. Every year IRCAD's remote surgery unit welcomes 3,000 surgeons from all over the world. At their disposal is an operating theatre with an array of computers. A miniature camera introduced into the body transmits images onto the computer screens. Surgeons do not touch patients. Remote technology enables a surgeon to operate on a patient who is metres away using voice recognition technology and robotics. It was the same principle applied to thousands of kilometres that enabled the Transatlantic Lindbergh operation.

Many other services and laboratories in Strasbourg's university hospital do distinguished work. Fields include medically assisted procreation and cochlear implants for deaf children. Recently the hospital's urology department and its biochemistry and molecular biology laboratory perfected a screening test for cancer of the bladder.

From the Astrological Clock to the Planetarium

In 1562 Conrad Dasypodius occupied the astronomy chair at the Academy of Strasbourg, the forerunner of the university. Between 1571 and 1574 he worked with the mathematician David Wolkenstein and the Schaffhouse clockmaker brothers, Josias and Isaac Habrecht to make Strasbourg's Astronomical Clock. All that remains today is the cabinet made by the cathedral's master craftsman, Hans-Thomann Uhlberger.

Between 1838 and 1842 Jean-Baptiste Schwilgué entirely reworked the clock's mechanism thanks to a brilliant rethinking of the complex mathematical ratios governing it. Every day admiring crowds flock to watch its clockwork automatons spring into action at 12.30: the stages of life march to meet death, the apostles file by and a cock crows.

The Astronomical Clock also tells several times: its silver hands show official European time, while the golden ones show local Strasbourg time or solar mean time, between which there is a half-hour difference. Apollo, Jupiter, Venus, Saturn and other deities in chariots drawn by real and imaginary beasts brandish arrows to indicate the days of the week on the perpetual calendar.

So marvellous are these features that enthusiasts could be forgiven for overlooking the clock's astronomy computation capability, which is really what makes it so special. Most remarkable of all is its automated, perpetual calculation of the year's ecclesiastical calendar, the first clock in the world to be able to do so. At midnight on 31st December, its mechanism goes into motion, determining the calendar

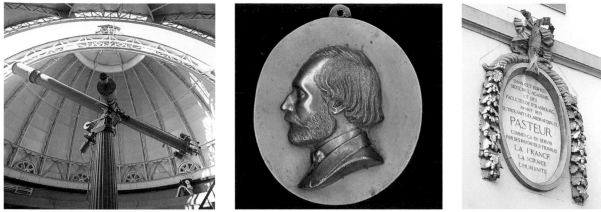

for the coming year, setting it in relation to the solar and lunar cycles and giving Easter's date. Its celestial globe boasts over 5,000 stars, its lunar globe shows the phases of the moon, and the planetary globe depicts the orbital paths of the planets around the sun.

Strasbourg's abiding passion for astronomy led in 1882 to the construction of an observatory in the gardens of the University of Strasbourg. Built by the architect Hermann Eggert, the main building is topped by a great iron dome which houses a seven-meter-long ray-gun-like telescope. When it was commissioned it was thought to be the world's most powerful. It is like being in a Jules Verne novel when the dome's panels slide open with a metallic grinding sound to reveal a great swathe of sky.

Nowadays astronomers have turned to the much more powerful capabilities of computer-driven technology. But there are still organized tours of the observatory for the general public and in 1981 it became home to the Strasbourg Planetarium, much appreciated for the way its makes science accessible. With its vast, star-studded canopy, whose mechanisms are designed to simulate the movements of heavenly bodies, the planetarium is a veritable space ship.

From Pasteur to biotechnology

Behind the railings of a school playground children are at play. On the main school building a plaque reads: "In this edifice, seat of the Academy and Faculties of Strasbourg until 1871, is the laboratory where Pasteur began to put his immortal work at the service of France, Science and Humanity." The address is 4 Rue de l'Académie – a trace of the time that Louis Pasteur spent in Strasbourg after arriving in 1848.

His six years in the city were busy indeed. Five months after arriving he wedded Marie-Anne, daughter of the university rector. He asked her father for her hand in a letter in which he modestly wrote: "All that I possess is good health, a good heart and a position in the university."

Three children would be born to the couple, who moved house several times. Plaques outside 3 bis Rue des Veaux and 18 Quai Saint-Nicolas, testify that they lived there. At the same time as lecturing at the Faculty of Chemistry where he became tenured professor in 1852, Pasteur also taught at the Faculty of Pharmacy. Says Professor Philippe Poindron of the faculty, which is now on the Illkirch campus: "Modern biotechnology was born with Pasteur and his celebrated work on molecular dissymmetry, which he carried out in Strasbourg. We can safely say that Alsace is the birthplace of biotechnologies. We are now in the era of knowledge of the genomes of living beings."

International recognition has gone to work carried out by the Strasbourg's Louis Pasteur University and research bodies like the Institute of Genetics and Molecular and Cellular Biology (IGBMC) created by Professor Pierre Chambon. Almost six hundred people work at the IGBMC. Its seven departments bring together wide-ranging disciplines and harness state-of-the-art technology in furtherance of the aim of understanding disease and sickness by first understanding how human genes function and organize. It is one of the few European bodies that studies humans, worms, flies, zebrafish and mice — the five genetic templates for multicellular organisms. The IGBMC's premises on the Illkirch campus was recently enlarged to include a new Institut Clinique de la Souris (Clinical Mouse Institute), a technological facility with a menagerie that can house up to seventy thousand mice.

Incubating Nobel Laureates

No less than sixteen Nobel Prize winners have taught or studied in Strasbourg. The first was Wilhelm Conrad Röntgen, physics laureate in 1901. He is still famous for his discovery of X-rays which are named after him. In 1952 Albert Schweitzer was awarded the Nobel Peace Prize. He had studied theology and medicine, subjects for which Strasbourg University was much renowned. In 1987 another Alsatian, Jean-Marie Lehn, won the chemistry prize for his work on "the development and use of molecules with structure-specific interactions of high selectivity".

Chemistry is one of Alsace's great strengths. It comes top in French league tables, with 12.2% of research chemists hailing from the region. In order to harness international chemistry research findings more efficiently in the search for practical applications,

Page left: *Albert Schweitzer preparing to leave for Africa.*
Facing, top down: *L. Schmug's 1904 fresco painting
in the ancient Cerf pharmacy; Contemporary footbridge for Isis;
Classical facade for the Strasbourg's teaching hospital.*

Professor Lehn initiated the Institut of Supramolecular Science and Engineering (ISIS), part of the Esplanade university campus. Designed by the architect Claude Vasconi, the huge building boasts laboratories for high-level doctoral research as well as more junior facilities for researchers who are just embarking on their careers.

It was also with beginners in mind that the entrepreneur incubator organization, Semia, was created. It serves Alsace-based university researchers, the National Scientific Research Centre (CNRS) and the Institute of Health and Medical Research (INSERM). The aim is to help them find business applications in leading-edge sectors like life sciences, chemistry, information and communication technology by of putting scientific research facilities at their disposal. Over a dozen companies are currently being incubated on the Illkirch campus.

Among the business projects that have materialised is Entomed, which makes and markets medicines based on insects' immune systems. Another example is Neuro3D, which specialises in the research and development of medication for the central nervous system, particularly for Alzheimer's disease.

The are plans to build a "bio-park", a business park providing facilities for fledgling bio-technology companies.

Strasbourg Worldwide

When there is an earthquake anywhere in the world, French journalists rush to interview experts from the Earth Sciences School and Observatory (EOST). For over 100 years seismology has been a Strasbourg speciality.

Another is astrophysics. Astrophysicists from all over the world use the "Simbad" data bank at Strasbourg Observatory. Created and maintained by the Astronomy Data Centre it is fed information by satellites and probes orbiting the earth. The centre

111

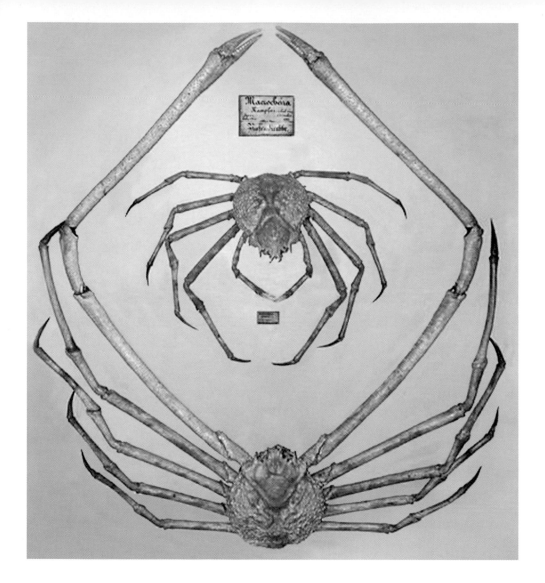

sorts and analyses data for publication on an international scale.

In late 2002 serious flooding swept southeast France. The Regional Department of Image Processing and Remote Detection (SERTIT) played an important role in tracking and assessing crisis data. SERTIT works in partnership with Strasbourg's Higher School of Physics (ENSPS) to process and read digital, radar and satellite data. A signatory of the International Charter of Space and Major Disasters, its expertise is sought-after worldwide when natural disasters strike.

Another example of the leading international role played by Strasbourg's scientists is to be found on the other side of the world, off the polar islands of Kerguelen and Crozet in the South Indian Ocean. The Centre for Ecology and Energy Physiology (CEPE), part of the Strasbourg branch of the CNRS has tagged king penguins there. The CEPE is tracking and studying the birds to see how their resistance to cold and ability to

store food could help in the fight against obesity and anorexia and, on a wider scale, whether they provide clues to global warming and the melting of the polar ice cap and how these impact on breeding.

Working in a very different sphere is a private laboratory, called Codgène, created by researchers from the Louis Pasteur University. It has designed DNA that have proved valuable in criminal investigations. Its best customer is the French Justice Ministry.

Strasbourg is also involved in ground-breaking initiatives. One is the International Space University (ISU). Originally created by a team of scientists from Boston in the US, its aim is to provide interdisciplinary, globally networked teaching for students and space professionals. Based in Strasbourg, which is twinned with Boston, the ISU's permanent headquarters are housed on the Illkirch Campus in a remarkable building designed by architects Archetype and Chouvet. Students come from all over the world. They

Page left: *These two* macrocheira kämpferi, *a species of giant spider crab, were caught in the Bay of Tokyo and brought to Strasbourg by Professor Döderlein in 1882.*
Facing, top: *Page from a herbarium book, a widespread passion in the 18th century.*
Below: *In the greenhouse of the botanical garden, the leaves of the giant Amazonian lily,* victoria regia, *can reach up to two metres in width.*

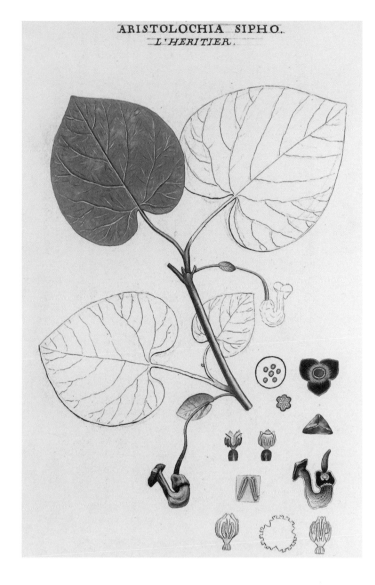

ARISTOLOCHIA SIPHO.
L'HERITIER.

either live on the campus while they study for their master's degree or attend summer school. Be they computer scientists or architects, recent graduates or seasoned professionals, the ISU offers an interdisciplinary approach to space studies that includes science, law, technology and ethics.

The Future Science Garden

Behind the old Palais Universitaire long swathes of greenery stretch as far as the Botanical Garden. On the edge of its small lake stand bald cypress trees, their roots thrusting up like stalagmites. Over 6,000 species of plant thrive in the garden. Some have been there since 1880, when it was founded.

It is said that the pagoda-shaped greenhouse, the only 19th century edifice to have survived, was designed and built to house the giant lily, *victoria regia*, which flowers but once a year. The greenhouse's metal structure distinguishes it from more recent constructions like the tropical greenhouse which houses plants from warm climes, such as palm trees, cotton plants, banana trees, cocoa plants and an amazing collection of cacti.

Flanking the garden are the Planetarium and Astronomy Observatory, whose dome can be seen from afar. The luxuriant setting gives science a romantic, escapist, passionate feel.

In the old earthquake measuring station that operated between 1900 and 1970 is a museum of seismology and terrestrial magnetism that is the only one of its kind in Europe. It contains a wide range of sophisticated oscillators and pendulums that can weigh up to 19 metric tons.

The Institute of Mineralogy has been home to a museum since 1890. It boast 30,000 exhibits from all over the world, including so-called "Rhine gold", a collection of gold-bearing minerals. Another curiosity is the pastel water colours of New Caledonian orchids that are conserved in the herbarium of the Botanic Institute. It has over 430,000 plants, the oldest of which date back to the Revolution.

Finally there is the Zoology Museum with its monumental entrance and sweeping staircase. It had its beginnings in the curiosity cabinet put together by Jean Hermann in the 18th century. Professor of medicine and natural history and director of the Botanical Garden, he knew many of the greatest scientists and scholars of the time. They would send him rare items and at times borrow from his extensive collections. Prize pieces included a stuffed wolf that had been killed in the nearby Brumath forest and a pair of gloves made from sea silk, i.e. the secretions from salt-water fish.

The Zoological Museum will be the core building at the heart of what is to be the "Garden of Science", a scientific museum complex that will show a wide range of knowledge and achievement. Its prime aim will be to highlight existing knowledge and to raise public awareness of science today. After conversion work has repurposed the Zoological Museum, it will also become a venue for debates and conferences with researchers and teachers on the state of scientific knowledge and the major issues facing humanity today.

It is an interpersonal approach that has been pioneered by three of Strasbourg's universities: Marc Bloch, Robert Schuman and Louis Pasteur. They have come together in a joint scientific and research effort, dubbed the European Pole, and organised a series of round table meetings with the public under the title "Savoirs en commun" (Knowledge in common). The venture has eased science out of the secrecy of the lab and boffins' symposiums into the living heart of the community at large.

7

Europe, a Fact
of Life

"I am European because I am Alsatian."
Pierre Pflimlin

Is Strasbourg a European city? Seen from an aeroplane the Europe of Strasbourg is a whole neighbourhood of imposing buildings set in an environment of water and greenery that run the gamut of geometrical shapes, reflective metals and iridescent translucency. The "European quarter" lies in the north of the city where the waters of the River Ill spill into the Marne-to-Rhine Canal, offering a magnificent vista from the buildings that stand along the banks. Europe is indeed a concrete reality, complete with its contemporary palaces.

White-on-blue signposts to the European institutions tell visitors arriving in the city that the union of Europe is being built here. All kinds of Euro signpost are to be seen in every street: "Eurocorps", "European Science Foundation", "European Audiovisual Observatory" and "Euro Ombudsman". Strasbourg shares with New York and Geneva the distinction of being the headquarters of an international organisation without being a state capital.

Aside from the institutions, Strasbourg hums with a special energy which springs from the fact that Europeans from countries all over the continent daily rub shoulders in the streets, restaurants, schools, universities and places of entertainment. The theatres show plays in languages other than French, the multicultural, French and German-language television channel Arte is based in Strasbourg, and restaurant menus feature a mouth-wateringly wide range of dishes and flavors. In the streets of the city buildings and bridges bear the signatures of Europe's leading architects and designers.

Its deeply rooted place in history and on the banks of the Rhine make Strasbourg a meeting point for the elected representatives, ministers and heads of state of a Europe that is growing steadily larger. The city lies at the core of a steadily growing, distinctively European culture that will be made of exchanges of ideas and experience, partnerships and coproductions.

In memory of Louise Weiss

The date was 9th December, 1918. On the "Kaiserplatz", now Place de la République, a grandstand had been erected. It was there, dressed in traditional Alsace costume, that Louise Weiss watched the "deannexation festivities, the commemoration of [Strasbourg's] return to France", as she noted in her diary. Originally from Strasbourg herself, the young journalist had come from Paris with her family for the celebration.

French General Gouraud had entered the city with his troops on 22nd November to a rapturous welcome. The people of Strasbourg were equally wildly enthusiastic when President Raymond Poincaré and prime minister Georges Clemenceau visited the city on 9th and 10th December, prompting Poincaré to state: "We have seen a plebiscite."

Louise Weiss had just launched a political review, *L'Europe nouvelle*. She watched the day's proceedings attentively, pondering the issues they raised for her as a committed pacifist. "Spahis [Senegalese and Algerian cavalry units in the French army], wearing their red fez were guarding the stands. I sat down slightly back from

Page left: Tomi Ungerer's posters for the 50th anniversary of the birth of the Council of Europe in 1994.
Above: The ex-libris of a work by Louise Weiss.

Raymond Poincaré and Georges Clemenceau… And a fantastic march-past ensured… It was like a torrent, a lava flow. Nobody had imagined such splendour or such passion. Was it worth the death of two million Frenchmen? That was not a thought that occurred to anyone," she wrote.

The young woman little suspected that her struggle for unity between peoples would see her many years hence addressing another assembly – the European Parliament in Strasbourg on 17th July, 1979. Her seniority earned her the privilege of delivering the inaugural address of what is still the only supranational body directly elected by the people. At 86 she began by expressing her joy, "the greatest joy a being can experience on the eve of her life, joy at the miraculous accomplishment of a youthful vocation."

The imposing building that houses the European Parliament is named after Louise Weiss. Completed in 1997, it will host MEPs (Members of the European Parliament) from 25 European Union member states by 2004. Seven hundred and thirty of them will meet monthly in the chamber, debating and voting on issues for a week at a time late into the night.

The birth of Europe

The great European venture had its roots in the aftermath of World War II. In 1946 in Zurich, Winston Churchill appealed resonantly for the creation of a "United States of Europe". Three years later in London, on 5th May, 1949, ten states signed the treaty which created the Council of Europe. They were Belgium, Denmark, France, the United Kingdom, Ireland, Italy, Luxembourg, Norway, the Netherlands and Sweden. Following a motion from the British Foreign Secretary, Ernest Bevin, Strasbourg was designated as the headquarters of the new institution even though it had not applied. For Bevin the choice of Strasbourg was self-evident: "The city of Strasbourg,

which throughout its long history has suffered as a bone of contention between the warring nations of Europe, will be converted into the centre of a new effort at conciliation and unity."

The city moved swiftly to make land available for the construction of the new Europe's buildings. In the interim, however, there was nowhere for the first meetings of the Council of Europe's two bodies, the Committee of Ministers and the Parliamentary Assembly. In the grand hall of the Hôtel de Ville (City Hall) on the Place Broglie, the Mayor of Strasbourg, Charles Frey, welcomed Robert Schuman, Ernest Bevin and other ministers of Foreign Affairs. On 10th August Edouard Herriot, the speaker of France's National Assembly entered the lecture hall of the Palais Universitaire to open the first session of the new European assembly.

The people of Strasbourg still remember Winston Churchill's vibrant speech from the balcony of the Aubette concert hall, which prompted great applause. After years of war and fighting, Europe had come of age in Strasbourg.

Since then the number of national flags fluttering in the wind outside the Council of Europe has steadily grown. In 2003 there were 45.

Human rights wardens

Hardly had it come into being than in 1950 the Council of Europe enthusiastically drew up its first great convention – "the European Convention for the Protection of Human Rights and Fundamental Freedoms". It did more than set out principles such as the Universal Declaration of Human Rights. It actually created an institutional system to ensure the respect of the rights it defined – the European Court of Human Rights.

Anyone who believes that their rights have been violated and has exhausted all avenues of redress in his

or her own country can take his or her case before this unique court. The number of magistrates matches the number of member states of the Council of Europe. All have lived and worked in Strasbourg since 1998 when it was decided the court should operate on a permanent basis and not just for one week per month as it did originally.

The magistrates wear mantles of blue – the colour of Europe – and their rulings override national law. Any member state that fails to comply is punishable by fine or has to change its legislation. The issues addressed by the judges, who act as wardens of human rights, range widely from press freedom to problems of eviction and people who want to know who their biological parents were. In the last 15 years the number of cases heard by the court had grown from 1,000 to 28,000.

Hearings are public, so those attending them also have the opportunity of discovering the new court building, the Palais des Droits de l'Homme, completed in 1995. It was designed by the British architect, Sir Richard Rogers, who also created the Lloyds building in London and (jointly) the Pompidou Centre in Paris. He envisioned it as a ship merging with the flow of the river. Two pink sandstone chimneys rise into the sky over the great vessel of a building made from translucent glass and metal panels.

A growing district

The Council of Europe estimates that more than 50 000 people visit it every year. The European Parliament's figure is 200,000. They are among the most popular tourist destinations in Strasbourg.

The Palais de l'Europe, which houses the council, is easy to spot. An imposing square block made of sandstone, glass and steel, it was built by French architect, Henry Bernard, in 1975. The interior is arranged around a vast mahogany panelled amphitheatre and enclosed gardens. Built on the edge

of the district of Robertsau on land donated by the city authorities, the Palais de l'Europe grows steadily.

Its recent extension has provided it with 22,000 square meters of conference halls and offices as well as new premises for the new European Pharmacopoeia. Not much in the public eye, the Pharmacopoeia nevertheless plays an important role in providing protection against error and fraud in the manufacture of drugs. It has also contributed to harmonising national standards and practices and validates testing methods for human and animal medicines.

The Architecture Studio which was involved in building the Institut du Monde Arabe in Paris designed the European Parliament, which was completed in 1998. It comprises two self-contained sections. One is a semi-circular building that gradually rises in height and whose great glass facade casts its reflection into the waters of the River Ill. It houses the 750-seat parliamentary chamber. The other section is a tower which houses MEPs' offices. Its facade curves around the sweep of a great square which solemnly

marks the entrance to the parliament. It draws on Galileo's circle and Kepler's ellipse to express the idea that the movement away from centralized power to democracy is a founding principle of Western civilisation. Over sixty metres high, the metal tower has an intentionally unfinished look that signifies that the union of Europe is still under construction.

The parliament already has plans for two new adjacent halls with a capacity of 450 and 24 simultaneous interpreters' booths.

In addition to the great symbolic edifices of the Palais de l'Europe, the Palais des Droits de l'Homme and the European Parliament that straddle the banks of the Ill, there are the four functional European Parliament buildings. Dark in color, they house offices and facility management services. A footbridge across the Ill directly links one of them to the Parliament.

Youth of Europe

The Council of Europe has a special building for its Youth and Sport Directorate. Located in Rue Pierre de Coubertin, the building's cubic architecture and luminous interior combine spareness of line with brut materials. It is characteristic of the rationalist style of the Swedish architects Lund and Slaatto who designed it. The European Youth Centre offers some 300 activities and organises numerous language learning trips and courses.

The involvement of young people is one of the spearheads of European construction. The main institutions have grasped this and organise major annual events in addition to more frequent smaller-scale ones. Thus it is that once a year in the courtroom of the Palais des Droits de l'Homme, the blue-mantled judges give way to students who compete in a plea contest held by the association, Juris Ludi. The cases tried are fictitious human rights breaches and the budding lawyers make their vibrant pleas only in

nous croyons en l'Europe

French – with English and Spanish accents. Nevertheless the passion that drives the contestants is the same as they defend rights such as those of binational children caught in tugs-of-love or women threatened with excision.

There is a change of scene for one of the longest-standing events aimed at the young and not so young. It is a course in human rights law held by the Insitute of Human Rights, which was founded by the 1965 Nobel Peace Prize Winner, René Cassin. Thousands of law students and young barristers entering the profession worldwide have attended the course, which takes place at the Law Faculty of Strasbourg. Whether they study or practise in Rome, Sao Paulo, New Delhi, Yaoundé or Cairo, it is a valuable opportunity for them to examine international and comparative law in relation to human rights. Each session addresses a different topic but always looks at intergovernmental organisations not just in Europe but in the Americas, Africa, Arabic countries and Asia. Humanitarian law, especially the role of the International Committee of the Red Cross, is regularly studied. The European Parliament regularly opens its doors to young people. It invites high school pupils worldwide to 20 total immersion sessions at the parliament – over 10,000 students per year. The Euroscola program simulates European Parliament debating session in several languages. The young MEPs meet and talk before flooding into the amphitheatre chamber for a plenary debating session.

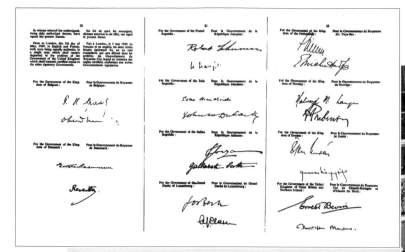

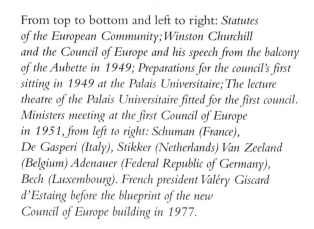

From top to bottom and left to right: *Statutes of the European Community; Winston Churchill and the Council of Europe and his speech from the balcony of the Aubette in 1949; Preparations for the council's first sitting in 1949 at the Palais Universitaire; The lecture theatre of the Palais Universitaire fitted for the first council. Ministers meeting at the first Council of Europe in 1951, from left to right: Schuman (France), De Gasperi (Italy), Stikker (Netherlands) Van Zeeland (Belgium) Adenauer (Federal Republic of Germany), Bech (Luxembourg). French president Valéry Giscard d'Estaing before the blueprint of the new Council of Europe building in 1977.*

Top down and left to right: *European Convention for the Protection of Human Rights; Bird's eye view of the Palais de l'Europe; Facade of the Palais de l'Europe; The magistrates from the European Court of Human Rights in session; Interior view of the Palais des Droits de l'Homme; The symbol of the 18ᵗʰ European Human Rights Contest; The chamber of the Council of Europe; Prizewinners; Palais des Droits de l'Homme, where the human rights court sits; The European Pharmacopoeia.*

Europe Daily

If you open a guide book to Strasbourg you will learn that the church of Saint-Thomas was founded in the Middle Ages by Irish monks, a Dutch sculptor introduced the vogue for pensive busts in the 16th century, a German cabinetmaker designed the library in the Palais Rohan and Italian stucco moulders produced its ceiling. The tokay wine that goes so well with the foie gras in the winstubs of Strasbourg comes from a grape imported from Hungary. Visitors crossing the city will see Irish pubs, Viennese patisseries, Swedish wooden toyshops, jewelers selling amber necklaces and bracelets from Russia, Lithuanian fashion boutiques, Greek and Italian restaurants and a Romanian delicatessen which offers a whirlwind culinary tour from the Mediterranean to the Baltic.

Some 1,700 international civil servants working for the Council of Europe have settled with their families in Strasbourg and made it their home. It is a fact of life which primary schools, high schools and universities have taken into consideration. At the Lycée International des Pontonniers, pupils can take the International Baccalaureate with options in English, Spanish, German, Italian and even Polish. Marc Bloch University teaches all the languages spoken by the member countries of the Council of Europe and the enlarged European Union.

Some "Euro-Alsatians" in the Council of Europe have been living in Strasbourg for over 50 years and have become deeply involved in the city's life – such as the retired councilor who teaches the art of cooking risotto at the Italian Cultural Centre and another one who organizes multicultural *stammtisch (regulars' table)*. Others run cultural and voluntary groups, organise concerts at home and exhibitions by artists from their home countries.

May 5th kicks off a whole series of "Open Days" during which the people of Strasbourg can visit the European institutions which have come to symbolise their city as much as the cathedral does.

Migrating MEPs

For four days every month European Parliament sessions are part and parcel of life in Strasbourg. They are heralded by the arrival of trucks that unload huge metal containers outside the parliament building. On the outside they bear office numbers and on the inside they hold the paperwork of the MEPs who shuttle between Strasbourg and Brussels, where the preparatory meetings for legislative work is done. The trundling sound of suitcases on castors can be heard in the pedestrian areas of the city centre. Hotels are packed both in central Strasbourg and on the edge of town.

Outside the parliament building there are bicycle rental points for cycling enthusiasts, who include numerous Dutch MEPs. But there is little chance to take excursionary breaks, as working sessions are long and hard and last until midnight. Most breaks are devoted to unveiling exhibitions designed to promote particular countries. Each MEP is entitled to organise events and to invite along fellow nationals as a way of publicising parts of Europe that are sometimes little known.

An amazing variety of languages and accents can be heard echoing in the corridors of the building. And with enlargement of the EU, that variety will grow even further. Thirteen countries are knocking at the door and in 2004 the European Parliament elections will include balloting in Cyprus, Estonia, Hungary, Latvia, Lithuania, Malta, Poland, the Czech Republic, Slovakia and Slovenia. In three years, Bulgaria and Romania will be joining, too.

It sometimes happens that a European Parliament session coincides with a Council of Europe Parliamentary Assembly, which takes place four times per annum, and even with a European Heads of State and Government Summit.

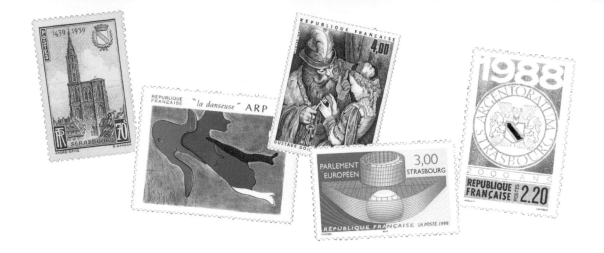

The Eden of Reconciliation

Strasbourg's Université des Sciences Juridiques bears the name of Robert Schuman. It was he who, in 1951, was the engine behind the creation of the European Coal and Steel Community (ESSC). The ESSC was accountable to a parliamentary assembly that was the forerunner of today's European Parliament.

Robert Schuman is an undying source of inspiration for the Mayor of Strasbourg and indefatigable advocate of the European cause, Pierre Pflimlin, who once said: "There is no doubt that here in Alsace the attachment to the European idea is more in hearts, minds and bodies than elsewhere. The declaration which Robert Schuman made on 9th May, 1950, was clear: Europe will unify on the basis of Franco-German cooperation. The European calling of Strasbourg is part of this context."

Today a Franco-German television team in Strasbourg edits and produces the nightly news on the transnational TV channel, Arte. It is headquartered in Strasbourg, from where it simultaneously broadcasts in several languages across Europe.

Another example of cross-Europe cooperation is the transnational army unit, Eurocorps. It is also based in Strasbourg and in addition to the French and German troops who originally constituted it, Spanish, Belgian and Luxembourg troops have now joined. During the May celebrations, the Eurocorps troops hoist their colours outside the Palais de l'Europe to the sounds of the European national anthem, Beethoven's Ode to Joy.

In the immediate aftermath of World War II, it was difficult to conceive that so much could be achieved so fast. Yet in 2002 a new bridge over the Rhine was completed – one more link between France and Germany. It has been named after Pierre Pflimlin. A Euro-district is being built between Strasbourg and nearby Ortenau, while along the Rhine the Jardin des Deux Rives (Gardens of Two Banks) is being built and landscaped.

A footbridge will connect the Strasbourg and Kehl sides of the garden. Inhabitants of both cities will linger to watch the water flowing under the bridge, before heading for the other side of the garden of reconciliation.

8

Art
de Vivre

"A touching sensuousness steeps the air one breathes."
Pierre Mac Orlan

Above: *Ensconced behind its walls, the Place du Marché-Gayot in the heart of the old city is reminiscent of an Italian piazza.*
Page right: *"A streetcar named pleasure."*

If Strasbourg was a flower it would be a magnolia – one of the pearl-white corollas that illuminate Place de la République and herald the arrival of spring. If Strasbourg was a color, it would be cathedral-pink, burnished by the rays of the setting sun. Were it a fruit, it would be a bunch of grapes, like the Gothic carvings on the jugs served in winstubs, where the wine of the year is celebrated with a handful of walnuts. Were it a fragrance, it would be the sweet smells of waffles, toffee apples, cinnamon and aniseed wafting over the Christmas street market. Strasbourg is a sensual, lusty city, an invitation to the rituals of the seasons – Christmas, Carnival, the Wine Harvest and summer's festivals. The streets bustle with activity even in winter when the steep-peaked roofs are capped with snow and the banks of the Ill sparkle with frost. The magic of the Christmas Market makes December the busiest tourist month of the year. In summer the city hums with happenings and music, its five hundred café terraces spill on to the street and the cathedral is draped in light at night. Translucent glass trams slip easily through the streets like great moving footpaths. Visitors riding them can take in the market on Place Broglie, picturesque rows of houses glimpsed from Saint Nicolas Bridge and Bernar Venet's sculpture, "Ligne Indéterminée", on the Place de Bordeaux.

Street Art

Strasbourg is indeed a city of contrasts. Its long heritage offers visions worthy of Vermeer side-by-side with works of contemporary art: the city is rooted in a region close to Switzerland and Germany whose bubbling creativity it shares. Some of its modern works are truly bold. They are to be seen not only at the Museum of Modern and Contemporary Art but also in the street, along the street car route and in public parks.

Crossing the city is like a treasure hunt: there are surprise rewards for the most attentive eyes, like bursts

of colour in the grey day. The hurried walker runs the risk of missing out on creations by internationally renowned artists that trigger the imagination. The European Centre for Contemporary Artistic Activities (CEAAC) has installed many of the major pieces.

When fine weather rolls around, Mac Adams's sculpture, "Meditation" can be seen daily at 12.30 in the gardens of the Palais Universitaire. The overall effect is that of a great metal compass. One leg, suggestive of the stem of a flower, bears trays on which stones have been placed. Another leg, or arm, lies flat on the ground. At its end is a flat, lotus leaf. At midday the stones cast their shadows on the lotus-leaf – but not just any shadows. Close scrutiny reveals a person meditating in the lotus position.

Another park worth a visit is the Parc de Pourtalès. It is a real sculpture garden, where seven works play hide-and-seek on the grass and in among the trees. The most famous are probably "Arbrorigènes" by Ernest Pignon-Ernest which mingles with tree branches and "Il bosco guarda e ascolta" by Claudio Parmiggiani, a scattering of great, surreal ears that listen to the forest. One work that is more difficult to spot is one by Jean-Marie Krauth, which consists of 130 tiny bronze figures arranged around a tree. There is also "Genius loci" by Giulio Paolini that is installed under a charm in the half-dark of the undergrowth.

A score of works have also been installed along the tramway route. Some are visual treats like the vividly coloured pedestals crowded with sculptures on the Esplanade. There is also a piece outside the Théâtre National de Strasbourg that is intended to encourage visitors to sit back and watch the city bustle by. Called the "Warburg Spiral", this bench-shaped sculpture is by Luxembourg artist Bert Theis.

Iranian sculptor, Siah Armajani, has designed a very Eiffel-like footbridge that crosses the river to the island called the Cité de l'Ill. People crossing cannot help looking down through the open metalwork to watch

the river flowing below. Armajani is also the creator of the "Gazebo" that stands by the entrance to Elsau Station. A reworking of the traditional summer pavilion, it has a table and benches and is topped by a 13-metre-high belvedere on which sits a green beacon that can be seen from afar.

Interiors

Visitors can also let their gaze wander over the city at leisure from inside the oriel window of an old Strasbourg residence that houses the Musée Alsacien, devoted to the traditional arts of Alsace. It looks out onto the imposing mass of the Ancienne Douane (Old Customs House) topped by a tall roof and criss-crossed with Medieval gables. It is easy to spend hours in the oriel just sitting on the sturdy benches or, chin in hand, at the table with its jigsawed legs and gazing outside. The Gothic vaulted ceiling and dark, carved panelling frame the view of the waterfront that unfolds like a painting beyond the sweep of the bay windows.

The Hôtel de Ville (City Hall) is on an altogether different scale. Built in 1736 by the Counts of Hanau-Lichtenberg as their private palace, its dining room now hosts wedding parties. The high, rocaille style ceiling decorated with masks representing the four corners of the globe and the red velvet seats produce a grandiose effect. The rooms upstairs have kept their white and gold Regency wood trimmings, the equal of anything in the Palais Rohan, built at the same time. Receptions and business meetings are now held there. Among the many fine 18th century works are two Gobelins tapestries, "Le Parnasse" (Parnassus) and "Les Adieux d'Hector" (Hector's Farewell), not to mention delightful, though less well-known artifacts such as the Chinese painted mirrors over the doors to the yellow room. They come from the old museum of the Cardinals of Rohan in the Château de Saverne.

Page left: *Outside the Law Faculty stands the* Grande baigneuse (2) *(Big Bather no. 2), sculpted by Emilio Greco in 1957.*
Right: *A door ajar offers a glimpse of the chandeliers and glittering gilt of a room in City Hall.*

The City of Strasbourg has also preserved the apartment rooms of Emperor Wilhelm and his wife, Empress Augusta, in the Palais du Rhin (Rhine Palace) almost exactly as they were. They are as different as different can be. The emperor's are decorated in an assertively German Renaissance style with wooden wall panels and ceiling embossed with plentiful imperial eagles. Augusta's sensibility was radically opposite. The well conserved boudoir is very Baroque in its inspiration. Callipygian cherubs frolic on a ceiling of celestial blue, while four figures vaunting traditional women's work and virtues grace the spandrels. A seamstress and embroideress face allegorical figures of motherhood and charity. Perhaps the most charming room of all is the former winter conservatory. Its French windows still open onto the garden outside and brightly colored birds still decorate it. They are peacocks, not eagles. The rooms once inhabited by the imperial couple and their guests are now the offices of the Regional Department of Cultural Affairs (DRAC).

Strasbourg railway station also possesses rooms which once welcomed the imperial couple. All that remains on the outside is the facade's corbelled window inlaid with neo-Gothic stained glass. The ceilings inside seem to sag under the heavy weight of their marquetry. The marble chimney, engraved windows and mosaiced floor complete the elaborate ensemble.

At the time, the waiting rooms – there were six – boasted luxuriant decoration. All the features that once bespoke the railway mythology dear to the 19th century, when a train journey was an adventure, have now vanished. *O tempora, o mores*. The eastern branch of the high-speed TGV rail network to Strasbourg is to see the station extended by a long glass-canopied concourse. TGV passengers will alight and depart in this huge, light-filled hall.

The Sixtine Chapel of Modern Art

Visitors keen to see a boldly creative interior should head for the Aubette music hall. Behind the classical facade of this stately 18th century building, once the guardsmen's barracks, lie the remains of an astounding masterpiece of modern art. Created in 1928 by Theo Van Doesburg, Jean-Hans Arp and Sophie Taeuber Arp, it was the first time in Strasbourg that modern art had become a setting in which people went about their lives rather than being a piece in a private collection or a museum.

The three artists designed and decorated a great four-storey leisure complex bringing together in one place a restaurant, bar, tearoom, cinema, dance room and billiards hall. The idea was that none should

overshadow the others, rather that each room and the activity it hosted should also invite people to move on to the next. That was Theo Van Doesburg's view when Strasbourg gave him the opportunity to put into practice the architectural philosophy he had set out at length in his review, *De Stijl*. The three artists sought to apply the Stijl doctrine upstairs and downstairs, using the straight lines and primary colors dear to Mondrian. It was only in the bar and the dance cellar that a little licence was allowed – the clouds painted by Jean-Hans Arp. This magisterial work had a lifespan of only 10 years. Times and tastes changed and the Aubette was redecorated shortly before World War II. It was no longer the interior design masterpiece that had prompted some to describe it as the "Sixtine Chapel of modern art". Happily, traces of the original design have survived successive renovation schemes and in 1985, the cinema-cum-dance-floor and its staircase became classified monuments. So did the ballroom and foyer-bar three years later.

The cinema-dance-floor has been restored to its former lustre. Its original decor has been replicated, complete with vivid colors, cinema screen and floor on which crazy Charlestons were danced. Everything has been painstakingly reproduced, down to the table nooks which, for Théo Van Doesburg, were as important as painting to the interplay of space and volumes. Restoration is ongoing and the rooms under renovation are scheduled to open to the public around 2006.

A conurbation laced with greenery

At the first rays of the summer sun the banks of the river Ill take on the look of a Sunday in the countryside. Students sit outside revising for their exams and families picnic under the watchful eye of the swans. Impassive anglers spend hours scrutinising the water. Exhausted tourists flop on to benches fanning themselves with their maps. Snapshot of a summer's day in Strasbourg.

With the high season the air fills with the scent of magnolias, lilacs or jennets which mingle with hints of river silt or mown grass. These fragrances waft over the city center and outskirts through which the Ill, as well as other rivers and tributaries like the Aar, the Bruche and Rhin Tortu (Twisted Rhine) all flow.

The Strasbourg conurbation is interlaced with stretches of greenery, where strollers can take unbroken walks for kilometers. The greenery links neighborhoods and stretches outside the city into surrounding towns.

Many of the waterways lead into parks. The Ziegelwasser – an arm of the Rhin Tortu – flows through the Meinau behind Schulmeister Park, named after its first owner, Napoleon Bonaparte's famous spy. It then runs along the Neudorf and through the little oasis of Kurgarten, literally the "curate's garden".

There are over 20 parks in Strasbourg. The biggest and best known is the Orangerie, with its alleys traced by Le Nôtre, its Josephine's Pavilion, lake and romantic setting. There are smaller ones, too, like Parc des Senteurs (Scent Park) in the Meinau district, which has plaques especially printed in Braille. And each has its own history, is special in its own way, and has its faithful strollers. The Parc du Contades is a favourite with some because of its bandstand and heady, early summer smell of lime blossom. Others prefer the martial feel of the Parc de la Citadelle and the Parc du Rhin, and others go for the rambling charm of the Jardin de l'Anguille (Eel Garden) in the Robertsau district.

On a much smaller scale are the allotment gardens that lie close to the parks, and which reflect the personalities of those who tend them. There is anything but monotony in these little 2.5-acre patches of land. Some boast pavilions, some magnificent flower beds, while in others exotic fruit grows together with traditional strawberries and gooseberries. There is infinite variety in the 4,700 gardens which form a *tachiste* patchwork, like an impressionist landscape, that delights walkers and cyclists alike.

Strasbourg shares this love of nature with Kehl, the neighboring town on the German side of the Rhine. Their joint passion has prompted them to design and landscape a 50-hectare garden on both sides of the Rhine, connected by a bridge for walkers and cyclists.

Forest on the edge of town

Not far away lies further pleasure for city-dwellers who like to get away from it all without getting too far away. The forest lies only five kilometers from the cathedral. And it is no ordinary forest – more like the Amazonian jungle. On both banks of the Rhine's alluvial forest grew in the early Quaternary Period in what is now the districts of Robertsau and Neuhof. The microclimate and special hydrographic conditions led to the growth of quite exceptional plant and animal life. Rhineland forest is unique in Europe in still having such remarkable and varied species of tree. There are almost 50 different kinds of tree, bush and creeper. Clematis and wild vine twist, turn and swarm up unabashedly to treetops 35 meters above ground. But if the forest is reminiscent of the jungle it is primarily because of its lianas and their formidable volutes.

Freshwater branches of the Rhine that had run dry have been revived in the Robertsau part of the forest. Bird-spotters can take boat rides and treat themselves to the astonishing profusion of bird species, over 200, more than half of which nest in the forest.

Rohrschollen Island, which prolongs Neuhof Forest, is where the most remarkably well conserved part of the forest lies. Energy utility, EDF, built a water-driven power plant there in 1970 and a new kind of industrial and ecological tourism has developed. After touring the power plant, visitors can then set off on a rambling tour which is signposted so that they miss out on none of the Rhine's special fauna and flora.

All these walks – through parks, along river banks and in the forest – lie only a short pushbike ride from a city that boasts over 400 kilometers of cycling lanes, bike parks and cycle rental points, where detailed maps are also available. Strasbourg is high on the leader board of France's cycle-friendly cities. The city authorities are planning to link the city's cycling lanes in an evenly distributed network across the city. They are keen to provide routes that are safe and convenient, like those along the Bruche, Marne-to-Rhine and Rhone-to-Rhine canals, where cyclists flock on Sundays.

Markets for all seasons

Every Saturday a dozen of farmers from the Vosges region set up their market stalls on the cobble stones of the Place du Marché Neuf. The market, a treat for curious gourmets, is the continuation of the market garden tradition on this little square that huddles in the shade of plane trees not far from a bustling shopping area of the city around the Rue des Orfèvres.

The market is sheer joy for the senses. Visitors and local people can revel in the sweet and subtle scents of honey, gentian syrup, blackberry macaroons and the lusty smells of fresh bacon and goats cheese. Traders' voices boom and ring: "Try my trout paté", "Taste a little glass of elderberry wine!" A trader selling "fat grey snails" offers snails skewered on kebabs, in pies and in their shells. There is every ingredient imaginable for a tasty, natural meal.

The market offers typical produce from the Bruche Valley and is but one example of the dozen or so markets that take place every Saturday in Strasbourg. They cater to every taste: there is the antique market near the History Museum, the Booksellers Market on Place Gutenberg and, of course, the food and arts-and-crafts markets. There are small markets, like the one that brings together only homegrown producers on the Place du Marché des Poissons (Fishmarket Square), a mere stone's throw from the Palais Rohan. There are big markets, like the one that takes place on Boulevard d'Anvers, where producers and retailers mix. All are held in the open air except for Neudorf Market, where the venue is the ground floor of a gigantic covered market built in the 1950s. Its upper floors are given over to a record library. Which sums up Strasbourg: shoppers can easily stop off for a little food for thought to borrow a book or CD or pop in to an exhibition. Every day, except Sunday, there are markets galore in the city center and outlying neighborhoods. The market that is held on Place Broglie always moves out in December to give way to the traditional Christmas market.

The fairy lights of Christmas

The Christmas Market ("Marché de Noël" or "Christkindelsmärik") dates back to the Middle Ages. At the time it was called the Saint Nicholas Fair. It started around 6th December and its stalls spread from the foot of the cathedral to the Rue Mercière. Traders

and craftsmen – e.g. potters, wood turners, locksmiths, armorers – showed their wares and skills to the crowds of city-dwellers and country folk who came from far around.

In the 16th century the Reformation almost put an end to this very Catholic market. It survived nevertheless, merely changing its date and name from Saint Nicolas to "Christkindelsmärik", i.e. the Christ Child Market. Interestingly, Christ the Child is depicted in Alsace as a young girl dressed in white and haloed in light, similar to Saint Lucie in Scandinavia. Standing next to him in popular imagery is the fearsome Hans Trapp, former companion of Saint Nicolas. He has the role of *Père Fouettard* – a bogeyman

counterpart to the good St Nicolas who brings nasty presents to naughty children.

Under its new name the Christkindelsmärik soon prospered. In the 18th century it became a cosmopolitan meeting point where the best produce from France, Italy, Germany and elsewhere was to be found. There were truffles from Perigord, meerschaum pipes and precious fabrics. In 1830, the market moved to Place Kléber, then on to Place Broglie in 1870. Its little wooden, shop-like stalls continue to sell the full range of Christmas paraphernalia, from Christmas tree decorations to coloured glass balls, carved wooden figures and sparklers, as well as the handmade gifts Alasatian people like to find at the foot of the Christmas tree.

The part of the market that sells resin-scented pine trees of all sizes and types extends from Place Broglie as far as the opera hall in one direction and the cathedral in another – so returning to the market to its original birthplace of centuries ago. From the wooden stalls the delicious fumes of mulled wine and cinnamon float up towards the cathedral like incense.

But Strasbourg's Christmas market does not stop there. The festive season is everywhere one goes. Stalls spring up on the Place Gutenberg, which is also the start place for the "tunnel of light", a star-spangled canopy of overhead lights which draws people on down the streets that lead off the square. Throughout December new attractions appear on every street corner tempting people on their way to and from the railway station, where other markets await them.

But Christmas is not complete without a tree and it is on Place Kléber that the biggest and most lavishly decorated stands. Crowds press in from all sides. A merry, joyful crowd warmed by the seasonal cheer.

A treat for taste buds

What would Christmas be without its aniseed *bredele* (biscuits), its gingerbread and other delicious pastries whose smells rise into the festive air of the city? Bakers' shop windows display chestnut torch cakes, a tempting seasonal favourite. But so it is all year round in this sweet-toothed city.

1st January is the day when the Strasbourgeois enjoy a *stolle*, a traditional German sweet loaf in four rounded sections that make it look like four-leaf clover. Then comes the *galette des rois*, a marzipan-filled Epiphany cake that is a nationwide fixture in France. With February come the carnival doughnuts. Plump, filled with jam and dusted with sugar, they grit between the teeth like sand before melting deliciously away. At Easter, shop windows suddenly teem with little lamb-shaped biscuits. Stuck into their icing-draped backs are tiny flags that show an emblem of Christ. There are also plain, white and crispy

Left: *Hannong's* Trompe-l'œil Dishes, *porcelain, between 1745-1754.*

Above: *Strasbourg illuminated.*

Pages 148-149: *All the wonders of a Lilliputian village on the Place de la Gare at Christmas.*

chocolate eggs, pink sugar rabbits and chocolate assortments, all of which hail Easter and the coming of spring. Also telling of the arrival of spring are chocolate hoverflies – scrumptious insects with black-striped backs, cardboard feelers and festooned with ribbons. It is now the rhubarb tart season. The season is short, so whether served with or without meringue, do not let the acid pink and green tarts pass you by. In July and August, as the city languishes in the heat of high summer, the pastry shops wheel out their ice-cream trolleys – which are instantly taken by storm. Ice-cream lovers relish the flavours on offer, which include all the fruit in the orchards of Alsace – and more besides.

The summer comes softly to an end as the gold of yellow plum tarts gives way to dark, glistening damson tarts dusted with cinnamon. Hardly have the people of Strasbourg had time to relish them than the first of the *maennele* have started to appear. These little gingerbread men with raisin eyes herald the coming of Saint Nicolas. The cycle of to-die-for cakes and pastries in Strasbourg is eternal.

Feast of friends

Be it the winstubs with their red checkered table cloths, smells of cooking ham and steamed-up windows which add to the good cheer, or the gourmet restaurants like the "Buerehiesel" and "Crocodile", the cuisine of Alsace is the most highly rated after Lyons. There are also the age-old brasseries and the very now places like the "Schutz" designed by architect Jean Nouvel.

There are of course places where people go just to be seen in – like any city anywhere. Winstubs work on exactly the opposite principle. All that matters is that the patron greets you like a regular, that the onion tart is cooked just right and that the jug of house wine is *süffig*, in other words light and fresh. Nothing else matters.

Winstubs date back to the construction of the cathedral, so it is hardly surprising that most of them are to be found in narrow winding streets around it. Some of the names are off-putting for French-speakers and can be found in the phone book in French

translation. For example the "Hailiche Graab" is also listed as "Saint Sépulcre" and the "Buerjerstuebel" as "Chez Yvonne". Some names are in a homely, reassuring French, while others like "Muensterstuewel" and "Zum Wynhaenel" take Parisians plenty of practice before they can say it properly.

The winstubs began their careers as outlets with a counter where wine growers brought their produce to be tasted. They then began offering plain, homely cooking to go with the tastings and some now have very extensive menus. Nevertheless, the reputation of a house hinges on the quality of its wine. The "Strissel", for example, promotes Hahnenberg wines, while Kientzheim vintages have pride of place at "Le Clou".

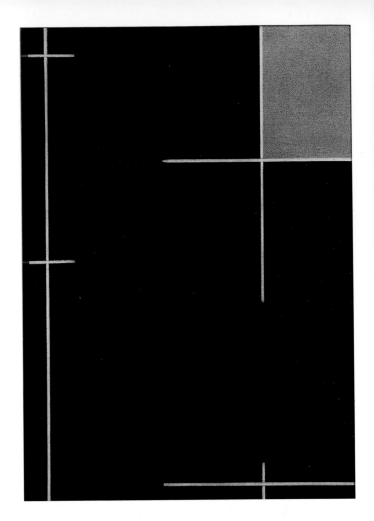

Although opening times vary according to the establishment, they all have one thing in common: Sunday closing. Winstub enthusiasts know which ones are open in the afternoon should they get a sudden hankering for a slice of foie gras or a dozen snails lavishly sprinkled with parsley.

Winstubs are unrivalled for their warm, friendly atmosphere. Nowhere else do people talk to each other across the tables, nowhere else are there so many different languages and accents – Italian, English, German, Scandinavian. And the people of Strasbourg – whether Strasbourgois born-and-bred or by adoption – all remain faithful to the deep-rooted tradition of gathering in a winstub on a set day at a set time around the *stammtisch*, i.e. the regulars' table.

Sun on the terrace, legends underground

Strasbourg boasts some 500 café terraces that spill out onto the sidewalks when the weather turns fine. Regulars know which are the warmest and brightest and how the sunshine fluctuates. Café terraces are where the natives mingle most freely with tourists. There they sit feeling as if they were on the Campo de Sienna or in a Vienna wine bar.

One place in particular is especially reminiscent of an Italian piazza. It is the Place du Marché-Gayot, a square not far from the cathedral that throngs with people night and day and yet still has secrets to yield. At the slightest ray of sun, people take pleasure in sitting out below the multicoloured awnings whether to enjoy a breakfast croissant or savour an early-evening drink. Now that it has been closed to traffic the old square has regained something of its 18th century feel.

The royal bursar Gayot had the square built in 1769, as a pink sandstone plaque testifies on the wall of a building which backs on to the Rue des Ecrivains (Writers' Street). The street has an 18th century house whose windows were once low and narrow. There is a legend that the dwarves of Cardinal du Rohan, whose palace was nearby, lived there. The story grew from there, the entire Place du Marché Gayot was by extension said to be riddled with underground tunnels the dwarves used to get about town. They would pass through the cellars of houses, many of whose ground floors today house oddly named restaurants.

Be that as it may, the Place du Marché Gayot is a favorite haunt of the city's young people. They meet there, revise their lessons, write, daydream, or thumb books they have picked up at a second-hand bookshop nearby.

A Culture of Culture

When the trees turn red and form golden canopies overhead, when chestnuts roll underfoot, autumn has arrived. The new season also ushers in the cultural season after a summer teeming with outdoor events. Brochures, flyers and hand-outs galore from the Opéra du Rhin, the Théâtre National de Strasbourg, the Théatre du Maillon, the Philharmonic, the Théâtre Jeune Public (youth theater), the Scala regional arts center, the Gare rock venue, the Odyssée cinema and more besides announce over 6,000 coming shows and events. Every page or poster is an invitation to come and discover new creations and premieres. They are often staged in Strasbourg before Paris or Brussels and include astonishing productions that rank among the best in Europe. The city is the birthplace of Jean-Hans Arp, one of the founding members of the Dadaist movement, and is also steeped in the satirical cabaret tradition of which Germain Muller's "Barabli" is still the unrivalled template 40 years on.

Strasbourg devotes more to the arts and culture than any other provincial city in France – 25% of its budget. The autumn is always ushered in by a business forum, the Foire Européenne. Hard on its heels comes Musica, a two-week contemporary music festival that has been running for 20 years. It is a mere fledgling compared to the International Classical Music Festival, Europe's oldest, which has taken place every June for 50 years. Musica has nevertheless forged an international reputation for itself and in 2003 it organised concerts all year long.

Strasbourg is distinctive for the sheer diversity of its artistic events, linked to the relative youth of its inhabitants, of whom over 60% are under 40. On the margins of the main concerts, stage productions and exhibitions that are publicised on banners across the city, there is a counter-culture of free or nearly-free events. Everybody gets to go out one way or the other. On one Sunday evening there was a Waldteufel concert in the auditorium of the Musée d'Art Moderne et Contemporain, an exhibition by one of the most startling Berlin-based artists at the Ecole des Arts Décoratifs, a Renoir film at the Maison de l'Image, a reading at the Italian Cultural Institute, a poetry evening at the municipal library, and recitals at the the Munsterhof. There was plenty for all tastes and for the curious, too. Utter bliss.

musica

Festival
international
des musiques
d'aujourd'hui
Strasbourg

21 SEPT > 7 OCT 2000

History in the Writing

Even as you read this book the urban landscape of Strasbourg will have continued changing in ways once unthinkable. Today the Franco-German border has blossomed into a park, the Jardin des Deux-Rives, and a Eurodistrict. In the heart of the city, meanwhile, united Europe is growing daily, just as it is on the world map. Toddlers are already taking their first steps on the Place Kléber, where greenery has been gradually reasserting itself.

The new ice rink will soon be completed and there, like in a Tolstoy novel, young people, their cheeks pink from the cold, will fall in love. Others will do the same in the heat of international sporting events at the Rhenus Sport stadium or in the dazzling light of laser beams in a concert at the Zenith music venue. Soon, too, the dockside district will host activities linked to books, music, dance, archives, science and technology.

With so many exciting improvements to the life of its inner and outer neighbourhoods, Strasbourg continues to write itself a place in history. It is a history that seeks to live up to the aspirations and dreams of the 21st century.

Contents

Acknowledgements

I would like to dedicate this book to all those who, in various fields, transmitted a little of their knowledge and much of their love of Strasbourg. They include Lucien Braun, Francis Bueb, Jean-Louis Faure, Georges Foessel, François-Joseph Fuchs, Jean-Richard Haeusser, Professor Jacques Héran, Professor Louis-François Hollender, Geneviève Honegger, Jean-Pierre Klein, Richard Kleinschmager, Françoise Lévy-Coblentz, Jean-Yves Mariotte, Roland Recht, Jean-Marc Seiler, Léon Strauss, Bernard Ungerer, Alfred Wahl, Jean Willer and, of course, Germain Muller.

I am also indebted to all those who helped me to write this book, especially Annie Dumoulin, François Miclo, Louis Nore, Jean-Charles Petitpierre and my colleagues from the City of Strasbourg, particularly the External Communication Department, who have given me valuable support.

My gratitude, too, to all those who provided me with documentation and pictures: Agathe Bischoff-Morales, Michèle Chirle, Yves Dirheimer, Paul Guérin, Emmanuel Guigon, Anny-Claire Haus, Fabrice Hergott, Alain Kuntzmann, Ernest Laemmel, Etienne Martin, Jean-Pierre Rieb, Bernadette Schnitzler, Christine Spéroni, Marie-Dominique Wandhammer, Nicole Wilsdorf, Thérèse Willer, Ellen Wuibaux.

Bibliography

History
Collective works
Livet, Georges and Rapp, Francis: "Histoire de Strasbourg des origines à nos jours", published by Editions des Dernières Nouvelles d'Alsace-Istra, Strasbourg, 1982.
Foessel, Georges; Klein, Jean-Pierre; Ludmann, Marie-France; Ludmann, Jean-Daniel; Faure, Jean-Louis: "Strasbourg – Panorama monumental et architectural des origines à 1914", published by Contades, Strasbourg, 1984.
Héran, Jacques: "Histoire de la Médecine à Strasbourg", published by Editions de La Nuée Bleue, Strasbourg, 1997.
Braun, Lucien: "Paracelse", published by Editions René Coeckelberghs, Lucerne / Lausanne, 1988.
Hollender, Louis-François and During-Hollender, Emmanuelle: "Chirurgiens et chirurgie à Strasbourg", published by Editions Coprur, Strasbourg, 2000.
Muller, Germain: "Strasbourg, ville de rencontres", published by Editions des Dernières Nouvelles d'Alsace, Strasbourg, 1979.
Recht, Roland: "La Cathédrale de Strasbourg", published by Editions de La Nuée Bleue, Strasbourg, 1993.

Biographies
Bailliard, Jean-Paul: "Kléber après Kléber", published by l'Association d'Alsace pour la conservation des monuments napoléoniens", Strasbourg, 1999.

Bechtel, Guy: "Gutenberg", Fayard, Paris, 1992.
Bertin, Célia: "Louise Weiss", published by Albin Michel, Paris, 1999.
Grossmann, Robert: "Le choix de Malraux", published by Editions de La Nuée Bleue, Strasbourg, 1997.

Travel writing and articles
De Nerval, Gérard: "Lorely. Cartes et facéties. Petits châteaux de Bohème", published by Imprimerie nationale, Paris, 1959.
Hugo, Victor: "Le Rhin", published by Bueb et Reumaux éditeurs, Strasbourg, 1980 and by Editions de La Nuée Bleue, Strasbourg, 2000.

Memoirs
Dumas, Alexandre: "Sur Nerval, nouveaux mémoires", published by Editions Complexe, Brussels, 1990.
Goethe, Johann Wolfgang: "Dichtung und Wahrheit"
Oberkirch, Baronne: "Mémoires", published by Editions Mercure de France, Paris, 1989.
Pflimlin, Pierre: "Mémoires d'un Européen de la IVᵉ à la Vᵉ République", Fayard, Paris, 1991.

Novels, poetry, essays
Arp, Jean: "Jours effeuillés", Gallimard, Paris, 1966.
Bachelard, Gaston: "La Terre et les rêveries de la volonté" published by Librairie José Corti, Paris, 1988.
Mac Orlan, Pierre: "Rues secrètes", published by Arléa, Paris, 1989.

Photo credits

© Adagp, Paris, 2003: Jean Cocteau p 121, Wassily Kandinsky p 152, Aurélie Nemours p 152, Sophie Taeuber-Arp p 138; © AIRDIASOL-Rothan: p 125; © A.M.S.: p 78-82 / Ernest Laemmel: p 107; © Belfort, Musée d'Art et d'Histoire: p 42; © B.M.S./ Ernest Laemmel: p 68, 76, 105; © B.N.U.S.: p 66-67, 109 bottom, 110, 113 top, 117, 121, 138 centre, 143 right; © Christophe Bourgeois: p 13 centre, 18-19, 21, 23 left, 24-25, 28, 38-39 right, 51, 53, 55h, 58, 71, 85 top and bottom right, 92, 95, 98, 109 right, 111 top and centre, 128, 131 bottom, 138 bottom, 145 top; the CEAAC implements these projects with the support of the Conseil Général du Bas-Rhin, Région Alsace, Ville de Strasbourg the DRAC Alsace © CEAAC /© Christophe Bourgeois: p 131 bottom /© Geneviève Engel: p 140-141 /© Klaus Stöber: p 131 top; © Council of Europe: p 118-120, 122-123; © C.U.S./Ernest Laemmel: p 109 centre, 126, 155; © Coll. Bibliothèque Alsatique du Crédit Mutuel: p 43, 48, 107 bottom right; © Franck Delhomme: p 100-101, 142-143 bottom, 155; © Doc S.R.A./P.Heckel: p 30; © Geneviève Engel: p 2, 10 to 12, 14 to 17, 20, 35 to 37, 39 left, 52, 55 bottom, 63, 73 to 75, 85 bottom left, 86 top, 90-91, 109 left, 111 bottom, 113 bottom, 128 to 130, 132, 134 to 137, 147 to 149, 155; © Fondation Arp, Clamart: p 138 bottom; © Fonds iconographique de la Fondation de l'Oeuvre-Notre-Dame: p 44 and 46 left and bottom right; © Musées de Strasbourg (D.R.): p 13 bottom, 23 right, 31, 32, 50, 61, 62 centre and right, 63, 65, 69, 72, 73, 77, 84, 86 centre, 87 top right, 89, 90-91, 94, 97, 109, 144 bottom, 145, 150, 152 /© E. Bacher: p 30 top /© Martine Beck Coppola: p 146 /© Christophe Bourgeois: p 45, 46 top right, 47 right, 151 /© Nicolas Fussler: p 13 top, 54 left, 62 left, 116 /© Juan Garc'a: p 152 /© Angèle Plisson: p 22, 29-30 centre 54 right, 59-60, 86 bottom, 87 bottom left, 88, 96, 138 top, 143 top left, 144 top /© C. Schohn: p 112 /© Frantisek Zvardon: p 47 left, 70 bottom; © C. Magelhaes and J. Coppens (D.R.): p 138; © Musica: p 155; © Mimmo Paladino, 2003: p 13; © PMVP/ Briant: p 93; © Jean-Pierre Rieb: p 104, 106; © R.M.N. / Le Mage: p 54; © Tomi Ungerer, 2003: p 116.